AN AUSSIE BACKPACKING LONDONER

1952-1953

GORDON J R SMITH

AN AUSSIE BACKPACKING LONDONER
1952 - 1953
Written and produced by the author Gordon J R Smith
Copyright © 2022 Gordon J R Smith

No part of this book and its contents may be reproduced for commercial publication in any form without the prior permission in writing from the author or a member of his family.

Email: gordon.smith9715@gmail.com

ISBN 978-0-6485390-3-2

Tale Publishing
Melbourne

Tale

CONTENTS

1 Introduction	1
2 Finding A Job And Full Board In London	5
3 Starting Work And Buying Some New Clothes	12
4 Back To Stevenage And Cutting A Record	18
5 Dancing At The Palais And Harrods	30
6 The Young Conservative Association And Fog	43
7 The New Year And Being Stood Up For A King	59
8 Touring Around England In Ralph's New Car	66
9 An Exciting Weekend In Stevenage	76
10 Dating Corinne An Elegant Date	81
11 The Cinema, The Ballet, Dancing And Football	87
12 Dating A Toni Twin And A Puzzling Noise	93
13 Ablutions And The End Of The Toni Twin	99
14 A Royal Funeral And To The Ballet	107
15 Easter In Stevenage	110
16 I Look For New Board	112
17 A Magical Night At The Ballet With The Wives	119
18 A *Comet* Crashes And The Aftermath	124
19 A Day At The Beach With The Yca	128
20 I Get A Call From My Mother	137
21 Coronation Eve And Saint Pauls Cathedral	142
22 The Queen's Coronation And Everest Climbed	148
23 Changing Jobs, Frank Sinatra And Sylvia	155
24 The Ballet, Weekends In Stevenage And Tv	160
25 Netta Returns To Australia	168
26 To The Ballet At The Royal Festival Hall	171
27 Exploring Bournemouth With Pam	174
28 Windsor Castle And A Thames River Cruise	179
29 A Musical End To My Last Weeks In England	184
About The Author	195
Books By The Author	196

Chapter 1
INTRODUCTION

An Aussie Backpacking Londoner 1952-1953* is a book from my daily diary entries about the wonderful eleven months I spent working and living in London after returning to England in October 1952, from my second backpacking tour. At the end of those eleven wonderful months as I had planned and had my passage booked, I set out on my last backpacking tour through France and Italy to join the *Orion* in Naples on September 18th to take me back home to Australia.

My aim while living in London was four-fold. To find a good job in my trade, find suitable full board and lodgings, enter the social life of London and to live as a 'Londoner' until after the Coronation, when I planned to return to Australia. I had no trouble finding a job in my trade and full board in Parson's Green, a couple of miles from the West End.

I was very happy that I had been able to settle into a working life in London so easily and quickly. Mrs. Banks my landlady looked after me like a son and very soon, I was accepted as one of the Banks family. Some food rationing was still in place, but Mrs. Banks fed me adequately with the ration tickets I passed over to her. I was lucky that Mrs. Banks had a TV set, which was a real bonus to my full board and great source of entertainment.

1

I began my social life dancing regularly at the Hammersmith Palais to the music of famous bands, including Victor Sylvester and Ted Heath, which I thoroughly enjoyed. I danced with many English and Irish girls, but none that I wanted to date, nor was dancing at the palais conducive to entering the social life of London. However, one day I saw an advertisement outside a shop looking for young people to join the Young Conservative Association (YCA). Despite my socialist bias, I immediately saw this as a path into the social life of London and straightway joined. So began my very enjoyable, busy, social life with the YCA and that of being a Londoner. I learned much about local government and business from guest speakers that from time to time the club had speak at club meetings.

During 1952 and 1953 many events of significance occurred not only in London, but around the world. The Great London Fog, the deaths of Stalin and the Dowager Queen Mary, Dwight D Eisenhower elected as President of the USA, the first commercial flights of the *Comet* and its subsequent crashes, the climbing of Mt Everest and the supreme event of all, the Coronation of Queen Elizabeth II. It was an exciting time to be in London and be part of some of these events and others. London is a wonderful city, especially for its theatres and entertainment venues, which I enjoyed to the full during the eleven months I lived there. The ballet, the movies and stage were my main interests in London. I regularly went to ballet performances at the Royal Opera House in Covent Garden and the Royal Festival Hall. I was thrilled watching the leading ballet dancers of the time, Margo Fonteyn, Alicia Markova, Brian Shaw, Anton Dolin and many others. I also attended the Henry Wood Prom concerts at the Royal Albert Hall. In this book I have described all the ballet, stage, screen and musical performances and venues I saw and visited in London, all of which have historical interest.

In London, Ralph Bateman an Aussie dentist was my constant companion, as was Netta Higgins, my Aussie Youth Hotel Association (YHA) Platonic lady friend, my regular date. We skied together for two weeks in Switzerland and found we had many interests in common apart from skiing. We went to the ballet, stage shows, the cinema and spent many hours together enjoying our mutual interests.

Ralph first introduced me into his circle of friends in Stevenage when I worked and lived there for three months after returning from my first tour. Some weekends I returned to Stevenage with Ralph to stay with my English friends. This was most enjoyable, taking me out of London for a pleasant change. I shared the driving of Ralph's new Ford Consul car when he went looking for a new dental practice in the south coast and Midlands of England. This allowed me to see more of the English countryside and its cities and beaches.

Every now and again I was invited to reunions of the Mt Buller, Aussie YHA members who were in London at the time, in fact unbelievably, there were 21. Some of these were nurses from the Royal Melbourne Hospital who found quite marvellous nursing assignments. Except for those very pleasurable meetings, all of my social contacts were English.

During the eleven months I lived in London, I dated many English, young ladies, some with widely contrasting personalities. Of note were Corrine, the assistant editor of *Harper's Bazaar,* one of the Toni Twins, a hair products model and a young YCA girl, who attached herself to me and caused me some concern. Every now and again I also dated one of our Aussie YHA girls. On one of these dates, she stood me up in favour of a King, King Hussein of Jordon! From these encounters and others I learned a lot about love, life and my own naivety.

Of course, the main highlight of my time in London was the Coronation of Queen Elizabeth II. Quite apart from the celebration and excitement of the spectacle I saw on Coronation day from my reserved seat in the grandstand, the lead up to the day was one of joyful anticipation of seeing the grandstands being erected, and the colourful decorations being strung up all over London's streets and buildings. The news about the climbing of Mt Everest that came through on Coronation morning was the 'icing on the cake' of the day. The Coronation was only one of the wonderful events that I experienced during my time abroad, but it was certainly the most spectacular event that I was ever to witness.

I worked for two English companies in London, the first a small company making electrically operated tools, the second a huge company, manufacturing military equipment large and small. In both of these companies, I did not have as close a relationship with the company or their product as I had at Kings in Stevenage.

When the time came for me to begin my journey home, I did so sadly with the knowledge that I had lived the life a Londoner, which gave me a valuable insight into the English lifestyle of those years and a love of London, the United kingdom and its people. The eleven months that I lived in London influenced my philosophy of life in so many rewarding and knowledgeable aspects in my journey through life.

*While I was living and working in England I did not participate in any backpacking tours, which is why this book is not included in my book, *Backpacking by Train in Europe 1952-1953*, but is a companion book completing the story of my time abroad.

Chapter 2
FINDING A JOB AND FULL BOARD IN LONDON

Thursday 2nd October 1952: I left the boarding house where I had spent the night and had breakfast in a café. I then rushed off to Australia House where sadly, there was no mail from my parents or from May, the 18 year old daughter of my distant relation, who I met in Scotland, or anyone else for that matter. While I was looking at various notices displayed in Australia House for the benefit of itinerant Australians, I saw an advertisement offering work for a fitter and turner at L and N Bridges in Parson's Green Lane Fulham. I suppose the company was aware that Australians were well qualified tradesmen, hence the advertisement there.

   I didn't waste any time in pursuit of the job, but first I purchased a very good street directory called *The A1 Geographical Atlas of London and Outer Suburbs,* which served me well all the time I was in London. I caught a double decker bus from Piccadilly Circus. About 3 km west along Fulham Road the bus let me off at Parson's Green Lane. I found a small frontage with a sign L and N BRIDGES PORTABLE ELECTRIC TOOLS above the front of the factory sandwiched between two dingy buildings, nothing like the big modern King's factory in Stevenage. I entered the building and told the receptionist in a very small office that I was answering an advertisement I saw in Australian House for a fitter and turner. I was directed to another small office, where I was interviewed by the manager of Bridges. I was not given any opportunity to see the inside of the factory, but I could hear familiar noises coming from machines. It was a very short interview and without any problems I was taken on, to commence work the following Monday at 7.30 a.m. in five days time.

So far everything seemed to be on a small scale, and so was Bridges the company, but I hoped that didn't extend to the wages. Bridges made portable, electric motor driven tools, such as drills, hedge clippers and other electrically operated workshop and general-purpose tools.

The next task was to try and find full board and lodging somewhere nearby. Most of the shops in the area had advertisements for all manner of things in their windows and outside their doors. Some of these were for rooms to let. I followed up on some, but most of them were small and unattractive, and didn't offer full board. I was about to give up and try again the next day, when I saw an advertisement for a room at 22 Chesilton Road in Parson's Green, offering full board. Number 22 was one of a number of residences in a row of terraced houses extending the full length of the street. The front door was reached through a gate in a solid iron fence that separated the front door from opening directly onto the path.

I knocked on the front door, which was opened by a middle aged, short lady, with reddish hair. I introduced myself and said I was looking for lodging with full board. She said her name was Mrs. Banks and invited me in to have a look at the room. She led me up a flight of stairs and into a large room where there was a double bed and fireplace. A large window in the room looked out onto a small backyard where there was an outside toilet. Mrs.

Banks then took me back downstairs to show me the dining room and kitchen. Next she showed me the bathroom that had a sink and a bath, with hot water supplied by a gas heater. So far, so good. For a change, the only small item here was the back yard, but certainly not the room she showed me. The house was only a 5 minute walk from Bridges, straight across Fulham Road. Fantastic, it was just what I wanted.

Mrs. Banks said the board was £2 per week paid in advance. I said I would take it and paid her £2 for the first weekly instalment. I gave her my ration book and said I would go and get my belongings and move in that afternoon. Mrs. Banks seemed to be a nice, homely person, in fact, she was to prove to be a good 'mother' to me for the next eleven months. I had noticed there was a small black and white TV in the dining room, which I thought would be beaut to watch.

Mrs. Banks gave me her full address.

22 Chesilton Road

Parsons Green

London SW6

Feeling very satisfied, I returned to my temporary board, paid my rent and went back to Chesilton Road with my belongings. Back at number 22, I settled into my room and unpacked, then went down the street to Fulham Road and found a place to develop and print all the rolls of film that I had taken on the tour. There were ten. I couldn't wait to see how they had all came out, but I had to wait three days before they would be ready.

My first dinner consisted of sausages and mash and a plate of jelly. The TV was on and as I ate I watched the news. Mrs. Banks said I was welcome to come down and watch the TV any time. There was also a phone, which Mrs. Banks said I could use if I paid her one shilling for each call. She said she was happy for me to give the number to my friends, so that they could ring me. *REN 2466*. It couldn't have been better and all so quick.

After dinner I took a bus and tube to Netta's flat in Clapham. Netta was very surprised to learn that I had found a job and board so quickly. I told Netta a little about my last tour and Netta told me what she has been doing while I was away. She had a very good job in London as a stenographer and had seen many good shows in the West End. I may have an inferiority complex, but Netta on the other hand is 'just a little too perfect.' We decided we would go to a show together soon. I said I would pick her up one day to show her 22 Chesilton Road.

Friday 3rd October 1952: I went to my bank in Berkeley Square and withdrew £20, which left £70 in my account. Then to Aussie House again, where this time there were a couple of letters for me, one from a lady in Denmark and one from May. May said she was longing to hear from me, which reminded me that I had hardly written to her or sent her a card while I was on my tour. The lady in Denmark was the one I had met on the Carlsberg tour. My mind was a little hazy about her, and I couldn't find any reference to her in my diary, not surprising considering the number of beers I drank on the tour that day.

I decided before I began work I would go and see my friends in Stevenage. I took the bus and along the way, I saw that many trees were displaying autumn leaves in all their beautiful colours. I visited Ralph in his surgery in Hitchin. He was delighted to see me and as Aussie as ever. I told him a little about my last tour and gave him my new address and phone number. He said that once I got settled, I must come up one Friday night and join them all again at the Brewhouse pub. Ralph was looking to find a practice in or around London, where he thought he would do better than in a regional city like Hitchin. "That would be really good to have you come to London." I said. I had left my golf clubs with Ralph to use while I was away, but said he could have them until I saw him again, as I was going to pick up my skis and case from the Bakers.

I walked to the Bakers from Ralph's surgery, which was a joy as the weather was not too cold and the sun shone a little. I got quite a good reception at the Bakers and had a nice cup of tea with them. I told them what I had been doing since I saw them last, which they seemed to find quite interesting. I enquired after Leon, who as usual was nowhere to be seen. Mr. Baker said Leon would be returning to Australia soon. I said to give him my regards and gave the Bakers my new address and phone number, and asked them to pass it on to Leon. After thanking them for all the help they had been to me, I picked up my case and skis and went back to London on the bus, arriving at number 22 just in time for dinner.

After dinner I watched the TV for a short while and then went up to my room to write letters to notify all my friends of my new circumstances, change of address and phone number, finally retiring to my nice comfortable double bed for a good night's sleep.

Saturday 4th October 1952: I rose early and had a breakfast of cereal, then went into London on a number 14 double decker bus. The journey took around 20 minutes along Fulham Road, past Walham Green and Fulham Broadway (the location of the TV *Minder* series). Fulham Road then turned to the left, and its name changed to Brompton Road as it continued on. From the top deck of the bus I saw Harrods, the famous department store. Brompton Road joined Kensington Road at Knightsbridge, entering the West End at Hyde Park Corner, passing by Mayfair and on to Piccadilly Circus in the heart of London, where I left the bus.

At Piccadilly Circus I found I could go down into the Underground to get to King's Cross or wherever else I wanted to go to. Instead of taking the bus to get into London, I could catch the train at Parson's Green on the District Line, but that was not as direct as the bus, nor did the trains run as frequently as the buses. Besides I loved viewing the life of London from the top deck of the bus. I walked down to Trafalgar Square and along the Strand to Australia House. Even at this time, over six months before the Coronation, I discovered I could book a seat in a grandstand, yet to be built. I put a £1 deposit on a seat to view the Coronation procession on 2nd June 1953, and re-registered my name with my new address.

Sunday 5th October 1952: Early in the afternoon I decided to take a walk along Fulham Road to have a look at the Thames and the township of Putney. It was cold and cloudy as I set off. After walking about 3 km along Fulham Road, lined with various shops and apartments, I came to the junction of Fulham Road and Fulham Palace Road. This led me across Putney Bridge and the Thames. The Thames flowing under Putney Bridge was roughly the same width and colour, a dirty grey as the Yarra, flowing under Princess Bridge in my home city of Melbourne.

The township of Putney is located just across the Thames. This Sunday it was quite busy, with a great selection of various shops, many of which were open. There was also a cinema with a small queue of people outside waiting to enter. I walked along both sides of the High Street in Putney for a short way. I then walked back towards Putney Bridge and passed a large hotel called The Star and Garter on the bank of the Thames. I returned to number 22 with the thought that the cinema, the hotel and the town of Putney, would be seeing some more of me during my time in Parson's Green.

After dinner I prepared for work the next morning and wrote a few more letters, especially one to May, then began sorting out some brochures and maps I had collected on the tour. One of these was the menu sheet of the Golden Adler restaurant in Innsbruck. This was where I had a very tasty meal and met an attractive widow called Annabelle. She said she was on her way to Holland. As we talked over a couple of drinks, she said that she would like to meet me in London. Annabelle told me she would be in London until October 5th and wrote her address in London on the menu.

I suddenly realised, that I had forgotten all about her and today, was to be her last day in London. But it was too late. I would certainly have liked to have seen her again and was sure that she really did want me to contact her, when I returned to London. With finding a job and board and all the things I had to do on my return, it had escaped my mind. I couldn't help wondering however, what would have transpired if I had kept the appointment.

Annabelle was very attractive, sophisticated and like me enjoyed travelling on her own. The short time we spent together in Innsbruck when I escorted her back to her flat and we kissed goodnight, gave me the feeling that there was a mutual attraction. As a widow, was she looking for another husband I wondered? I am quite sure that if I had met her, I would have wanted to continue seeing her. Where that would have led us if anywhere, I am not sure. Why I didn't follow up the address she gave me to see if I could contact her, I don't know. Pity, but she was 'just another ship that passed in the night.'

Chapter 3
STARTING WORK AND BUYING SOME NEW CLOTHES

Monday 6th October 1952: I lined up outside the doors of Bridge's factory at 7.30 a.m. with a motley collection of men and women employees. When the factory doors opened I was directed to an office where I was interviewed by the foreman who introduced himself as Jack Adams. We shook hands and he told me the hours were 7.30 a.m. to 5 p.m. with a lunch break to make up 44 hours. I would be paid three shillings and four pence (3/4) per hour. He asked me to sign a form and took me into a workshop to begin work on a milling machine.

I was quite familiar with the operation of a milling machine, having used them many times in the Victorian Railways (VR). The work piece is held stationary in the milling machine vice, while a revolving cutter removes metal, the exact opposite of a lathe, where the work piece revolves and the cutting tool is held tightly in a tool holder.

Bridges was nothing like Kings as a workplace. It was small, dimly lit and the milling machine was old and in poor condition. It was quite a new experience for me to have women working on other machines alongside, but I would have to get used to that. I knew that women working in industry had been quite common during the war, so I imagined this was a natural legacy of those years. I was introduced to some of my work mates including the women during the morning tea break. They seemed to be a good lot and were very interested to learn that I was an Australian.

My first work day at Bridges was one of adjusting to a working environment that was so unlike the work conditions I had experienced at Kings, or for that matter back in Australia, where we enjoyed a 40 hour week. As regards the hourly rate I couldn't compare it with Kings, because I never really knew what it was, however when I receive my first pay packet it will be revealed.

Before I went to bed that night I phoned Glasgow and talked to May, Uncle John and Auntie Greta. They said they would send my case to King's Cross in the morning. I could expect to pick it up there in a couple of days. I thanked them for their trouble, and finished the call talking to May about my trip.

Tuesday 7th October 1952: On my second day at Bridges, I settled into my new job, enjoying the work, despite the poor state of the machine. After work I picked up my developed films from the tour, and was devastated to discover that light had been getting into the camera damaging many of the photos. That was a big disappointment, but I sorted them all out and thought that I would be able to salvage many of them to provide me with some record of my tour. I would have to buy a new camera, but I had to admit that the Kodak Baby Brownie, a present given to me in 1944 had served me well.

In the year 2000, my son Graham cajoled me into writing about my two years abroad, and set me up with a computer, printer and Photoshop. I began writing and have not stopped since that time. I began learning to use Photoshop and finally became proficient enough in its use to begin repairing the light damaged photos. I found that literally, only a couple were beyond repair, as can be

13

seen in this book.

Wednesday 8th October 1952: Today could be called a 'crashing day.' First of all, when I got home from work there was a letter from my mother, passed on from Australia House. Amongst many good news items, there was one that was not good at all. It was about Roy, my best friend back in Australia, who had an accident driving up the mountain road to Mt Buller. Roy was on his way to the YHA chalet in his car, a two-seater soft-top Vauxhall, when somehow he drove over the side of the road. He was badly injured. He lay beside the car until the next morning, when a passing motorist heard his cries for help and he was rescued. He sustained a badly broken leg and some minor injuries. I rang Netta straight away and told her the news. There was a letter too from May in which she wrote that her sister Heather was very ill. This was very sad news indeed.

The next crash I learned about was when I saw on TV, scenes of a huge, railway accident at the Harrow and Wealdstone railway station in the north of London. 112 persons were killed and 150 injured. It was the worst railway accident in England. The crash occurred when the double-headed, 15 coach, Euston to Liverpool express train running at 90 km/h, was approaching the station. A little further down the line another steam train bound for Perth, had ignored a stop signal and crashed into the rear of a stationary, local train. This derailed the locomotive of the Perth train, into the path of the Euston to Liverpool express, which resulted in a catastrophic head-on collision. The crash scenes on TV were horrific.

Thursday 9th October 1952: I got a phone call from King's Cross station saying that my case had arrived from Scotland, so after dinner I went and collected it. It was great to have a few more clothes to wear and other odds and ends.

Friday 10th October 1952: My first week at Bridges went by very quickly. Today I got my first Bridges pay packet. I didn't know why, but I received a £1 bonus, making my pay for the week £6/10. This meant that without the bonus, I was £2 down on my week's wage from Kings, which was not the best, but even so I decided to live with it and see if I could save a bit.

After dinner, I rang Netta and invited her over. Netta said that my good friend Lionel was coming to visit her that evening, so I said to bring him too. It was great to see Lionel again after running into him by accident in Cambridge. They liked my room and we had a great talk together. After they left Mrs. Banks said they were both very nice Australians.

Saturday 11th October 1952: I decided I didn't want to be a hobo while I was living in London. I wanted to be well dressed. I decided to 'damn the expense' and buy some good clothes. I went into the West End and bought a tie clip for 35 shillings, a shirt for 35 shillings and an overcoat for £15. By this time I was nearly out of money but what the hell. I had myself measured for a single breasted, navy blue suit. I had always worn double breasted suits, but now single breasted suits were in fashion. The days were getting shorter and quite cold, a different cold from that at home, biting and invasive, so I had a real need for a good overcoat if nothing else.

The coat I bought was a beautiful, heavy, grey and white herringbone, lined inside with a blue grey and white, plaid material. It had fitted shoulders and was lovely and warm. I was a little undecided at first about the style of overcoat to buy, because I was quite taken with the beige duffle coats with a hood, with wooden button toggles that some of the crew wore on the *Moreton Bay*. They looked wonderfully warm and practical, but in the end I decided on the more elegant overcoat, set off with a beige scarf. I was hoping somehow to enter the social life of London if the opportunity arose, so I needed to have good clothes.

I had achieved my first two aims very easily, that of finding a job and full board. My next aim was to join the social life of London just as I had at Stevenage. I was not sure how to bring this about. In London there were many YHA Australians living in around London, who I had already met. All close and valuable friends, some of whom were living together in flats, as were the nurses. Others were scattered around London in various types of accommodation, 'digs' as they are called in England. I knew I would be welcome to join them in their social activities, but no, I wanted to *live the life of a Londoner* while I was in London. How I was going to achieve this life style I wasn't sure, but hoped it would be as easy as in Stevenage.

Sunday 12th October 1952: I met Mrs. Banks's daughter Sylvia and her Welsh husband Gwyn Jones. Sylvia looked very like the actress Vivienne Leigh. She worked at Harrods and Gwyn was a bank manager. They were on their way to a house that they were to about to move into. They asked me if I would like to come to their house after lunch to help them hang their curtains? I was surprised and flattered by the invitation as I had only just met them. I quickly said "I would love to." Mrs. Banks must have told them previously that her new boarder was a good fellow. Gwyn and Sylvia's house was in Wimbledon. They gave me directions how to get there, and after lunch I caught the train at Parson's Green, third-rail electric, which went a couple of stations further out along the District line to Wimbledon Park. I found their new stylish house easily and had a very pleasant afternoon helping Sylvia and Gwyn with their curtains. They are a really elegant couple and I enjoyed being with them.

When I returned to number 22, Mrs. Banks introduced me to her two new boarders, Mr. and Mrs. Cornish, a middle aged couple who were moving into another room. Mr. and Mrs. Cornish wouldn't be affecting me too much, because the room they were moving into was upstairs above mine, and was completely self-contained. I was surprised to learn that number 22 was much larger than I imagined, in fact I just realised it had three floors.

Monday 13th October 1952: After a very pleasant weekend I began my second week working for Bridges, which sadly was not destined to be as straightforward as the first. My foreman advised me that I was going to be working on 'piece-work,' a method of assessment and payment that most of the other workers at Bridges were on. I would still be on my hourly rate, which amounted to £7/3 per week before tax. I would be set a quota for each job I was working on, and on Friday pay day of each week, I would be notified of my week's efficiency with my pay being adjusted accordingly.

The working conditions at Bridges were not good. Apart from the poor condition of the machines, there was a lack of adequate lighting, which was not only dangerous, but was not conducive to working efficiently. The factory was also poorly ventilated, and there were no lockers for the employees to store their clothing and other odds and ends. What was needed at Bridges I believed was a good dose of unionism with a capital U! I was tempted to look for a new job, but considered that I probably wouldn't have earned any more elsewhere and very importantly, Bridges was so handy to my board, which is excellent.

Chapter 4
BACK TO STEVENAGE AND CUTTING A RECORD

'Ma Banks' or just 'Ma,' as I now call Mrs. Banks was looking after me like a mother. She said that girls were not allowed in my room, which I thought to myself was a shocking waste of a double bed. However, her prohibition was probably for the best as it turned out.

Tuesday 14th October 1952: I was working on a piece-work job when my foreman Jack, asked me to do some work rectifying parts that another employee had buggered up. He said this work was not on piece-work, although I was sure the original work had been on this basis. Any company using piece-work as a method of increasing its productivity needs to have very good quality control, but I had seen no evidence of this at Bridges. The work I was asked to do I was sure, was a result of this omission.

Ralph rang and asked me if I could come up next Friday night to Stevenage and stay at Brian and Sheila's for the night? I said that would be great. I told Ma Banks of my plans and prepared to leave London straight after work on Friday night.

Wednesday 15th October 1952: During the week I received many letters from my parents and a few from YHA friends that had been sent on from Australia House. They were all a joy to read and brought me up to date with the events at home. There was also a letter from May saying that Heather had hepatitis and her health was deteriorating. That was very sad news. There was another item of mail that Mrs. Banks had signed for and paid £2 customs duty. I paid Ma Banks back right away and opened the small parcel.

It was an electric razor. It had been sent to me as a sample from the Austrian firm of Payer, who had acted on the interest I had shown in their product at the Hannover trade exhibition. I tried it out, but I didn't like shaving dry. It could however, come in handy for a quick shave every now and again. Now that I was living in London I decided to write to Judy my former Aussie girlfriend, and give her my address and phone number, to see if we could get together again as I had not seen her since I left on my last tour.

Thursday 16th October 1952: After working on many of the faulty parts for a couple of days, my foreman said that it wasn't worth trying to rectify them all. It was found that only 30% were faulty and the rest would be scrapped. I reverted to my former job on piece-work, hoping that I could make some extra money. Ralph rang to tell me to meet him and my friends 'the mob' in the Bell Inn, a pub in Codicote and explained to me how to get there.

Friday 17th October1952: I couldn't believe it when I received my pay and found I had been accorded an efficiency of 120%. I felt that they must have taken into account the work I had done on the faulty parts, even though it was to no avail. Straight after work I hurried back to number 22, changed into my good clothes, picked up a bag with my overnight things and said goodbye to Ma Banks. I went in to the West End, had a ham sandwich and caught a green, Birch bus (a private bus company) that went through Watford and St Albans to Codicote, a small town north west of Welwyn. I found The Bell Inn where the group were already there and well primed up. It was great to see them all again and after kisses and handshakes, I settled down to some serious drinking. It was quite a shock to be drinking room temperature English beer again, after drinking so many excellent tasting, cold beers during my last tour.

Of course they all wanted to know about my tour, so I showed them some of my photos, which even though some were light spoiled they found very interesting. They shared my disappointment with the faulty camera. Marie my first English girl friend was there looking lovely, and we had a pleasant talk together. After a wonderful night Brian and Sheila drove me to their place in Stevenage where I spent the night.

Saturday 18th October 1952: After a hearty breakfast of bacon, eggs and tomatoes, I collected the records I had left with Brian and Sheila, except a few of their favourites, which I gave them. They drove me to the bus stop, where I thanked them. They said "You must come up and visit us again soon."

I had a slight hangover as I boarded the bus on the way back to London. Thinking about the visit, I was glad I was no longer a part of the Friday night 'wind down' with the mob, but I had to admit it was wonderful while it lasted. I was very pleased that Ralph had invited me to meet all my good friends at Stevenage so soon after settling in London, because it meant that I would still be involved in the social life of England in Stevenage.

As soon as the bus arrived in London, I went to number 22 and had my lunch and went back into the West End. Daylight saving was over so the hours of daylight were becoming shorter and the days much colder. I loved London and was quickly learning to find my way round by tube and bus.

I bought a new camera, another Kodak, which cost £3/15. The camera was more modern and better quality than my former one, but was still only capable of taking eight photos on a roll of film.

This was, however, quite usual for cameras of that time. The chemist shop where I bought the camera didn't have a case for it, but I found a case with a carrying strap in another shop. Next I went to Australia House, where amongst other interesting things, I discovered that it was possible to make a personal recording of a message on a 12-inch 78 rpm disc at His Master's Voice (HMV) in Oxford Street, and they would post it back to Australia.

I thought it was a great idea and decided to arrange to make one. Last of all I picked up my new suit at the tailors in Shaftesbury Avenue off Piccadilly. I was very pleased. It looked great and fitted perfectly, the first time I had ever worn a single-breasted suit. Strangely, I did not note the price down in my diary, but I think it was about the same cost as the overcoat, £15. By this time I was worn out. It had been a long day, but I wasn't too tired as I made my way back to number 22, to enjoy seeing many women in London wearing knee high boots, especially attractive when worn with a short skirt.

Sunday 19th October 1952: I had dinner with friends of Ma Banks, Paddy, Audrey and little Jackie, nice people. Then I went with Ma to Putney where I met her other daughter Barbara, not as beautiful as Sylvia and her 5-year-old son Brian, a little bugger. Also there was Auntie Maude nice middle age lady. I had tea with them and learned that Barbara's husband was on business in South Africa.

We came back home and watched What's My Line? A very popular TV show hosted by Aemon Andrews, a famous TV personality. It brought people into the show who had unusual occupations. There was a panel of celebrities, including a grumpy, old, English broadcaster Gilbert Harding and Barbara Kelly, a vivacious actress. The panel was required to deduce the occupation of the contestants by asking a limited number of questions, to which the answer could only be 'Yes' or 'No.' It was an interesting and very enjoyable show not only because of the celebrities on the panel, but also because of the obscure occupations revealed by the contestants.

Then we watched a film about Neville Duke, Hawker's chief test pilot, the first RAF pilot to break the sound barrier. He had accomplished this record in a Hawker Hunter aircraft, in a dive at the Farnborough Air Show the previous April. The documentary portrayed the life of this famous test pilot and his dangerous, but rewarding occupation, which was truly enthralling. BBC TV has many great shows. It was so wonderful that Ma Banks had a TV and I was able to see so many, interesting shows on the small, 12 inch, black and white screen.

Monday 20th October 1952: Back at Bridges I was once again asked to rectify work on a flat rate, which another chap has buggered up on bonus. When I was working at Kings, my skill as a tradesman was recognised and I was offered advancement, but at Bridges, the exact opposite seemed to be occurring. The type of work I was doing on the milling machine did not take a lot of skill, but working on an old, worn out, defective machine, certainly did.

Wednesday 22nd October 1952: During the week I made notes of what I wanted to record on the disc at HMV, then rang up and made an appointment for Saturday 25th October at 10 a.m. I received a letter from Walter Holz, the German skier I toured with around the Matterhorn. I had written from Amsterdam, telling him I had passed near where he lived on my way to the Rhine. He was very sorry I hadn't been able to call in to see him. Another letter was from Mac, my good, Cockney, merchant navy friend from Kings, saying that he would be in London next Saturday afternoon.

Would it would be OK to visit me at number 22. I wrote straight back saying that I would be looking forward to his visit.

After dinner I went out to Lionel's digs with Netta and spent a boring evening. I seemed to be making all the conversation. My relationship with Netta was an interesting one, not one of romantic interest, but she was a good friend and we both had similar interests. I wasn't sure if she still thought I had an inferiority complex, but lately she was becoming something of a know all.

Friday 24th October 1952: I began working on a new job, which I hoped would make me some cash, and it did. At the end of the week, I not only received a respectable work percentage of 101%, but also a £5/10 tax refund. Before I went to bed, I completed my notes of what I wished to say on the record.

Saturday 25th October 1952: I went to HMV, a large shop in Oxford Street for my 10 a.m. appointment to make the recording to be sent back home. I had been to HMV once before to buy records. I was directed to a recording booth at the rear of the shop, where I was seated in front of a microphone. When I was ready, I was told to begin talking as soon as the red light in front of me was illuminated. I wasn't a bit nervous, and when the light came on, I began to read from my notes, first about the time I had spent in Glasgow. There was a timer in my view that indicated the elapsed time, but I don't think I was aware of it.

I talked about how I missed the family and loved them and to not worry about me, I was getting on OK. The light went out before I had said everything I wanted to say, but I managed to talk about 90% of what I had written, so I was quite pleased. I gave the address of my home in Rosanna and paid £10, which included packing and mailing to Australia. I thought it was good value for £10.

Amongst a variety of sound systems and records on display in the HMV shop, I saw a portable record player housed in a solid, maroon, Bakelite case with a carrying handle. It was just what I wanted, so I bought it and walked out of HMV very happy with my new purchase onto bustling Oxford Street. Oxford Street reminded me very much of Bourke Street, Melbourne. Bourke Street, like Oxford Street, was one of the main shopping streets of the city. Both streets have a large shopping emporium, Selfridges in Oxford Street and Myer in Bourke Street. I returned to number 22 and played a few records on my new player while I waited for Mac. The record player worked very well and sounded quite good, so I was thrilled.

Mac arrived soon after lunch. It was great to see him again. He brought me up to date with all the happenings at Kings, and I told him about the trials and tribulations of my new job at Bridges. How different it was from the working conditions at Kings. Mac was a very good friend to me while I was in Stevenage. I appreciated his friendship when I was getting to know the ways of the English working man. Ma Banks made us a cup of afternoon tea and I was very pleased because she and Mac made quite a hit together. We watched TV for a while and then it was time for Mac to leave, having vowed to keep in touch with each other.

Sunday 26th October 1952: I rang Joan Cooper an Australian nurse and invited her to spend the afternoon with me in London and go to a show. I arranged to meet her at Piccadilly Circus tube station. Joan is an attractive and happy person, one of a group of three Royal Melbourne Hospital nurses, Rosemary Roberts, Joan Cooper and June Lucas, who was on a ship to the UK and would be in London in a month or so. I visited Rosemary and Joan in London before I went on my last tour. I met the three nurses in YHA and went together with them on many skiing and other trips. I dated June Lucas, an elegant brunette on a number of occasions.

I met Joan and we decided to go and see the Coronation robes in Kensington Palace. We took a bus out past Hyde Park Corner to Kensington Gardens and walked a short distance to Kensington Palace. The palace looked just like a large rectangular, residential building, with big windows all along the front. Although the building itself looked very plain, the Coronation robes and crown inside, were anything but plain. The robes were very beautiful in purple, gold and white, fur lined fabric. There was an imitation crown, which looked very heavy as it had a lot of precious stones all over it. Many members of the Royal Family lived and died in Kensington Palace. It was Princess Diana's home until she was killed in Paris on 31st August 1997,

We were both very aware of how fortunate we were that we would be in London next year for the Coronation. Leaving the palace, we returned to the West End and went to the cinema, where we saw *The Planters Life* that had just been released, starring Claudette and Jack Hawkins, a very good movie about terrorism, in Malaya. After the cinema we had dinner in town and talked about the great times we had had skiing, hiking and going on trips with YHA, and how lucky we were to have the opportunity to travel to the UK and live in the wonderful city of London.

I took Joan back to her flat in Notting Hill Gate, where I met Rosemary and a couple of other nurses. Australian nurses were in great demand in the UK because they possessed very good qualifications. The nurses had all joined a nursing agency, which provided them with many interesting and unique assignments. Joan and I enjoyed our day out together, so much so that we decided to do it again soon. We parted with a kiss.

Fulham Road just before it becomes Brompton Road

My new home 22 Chesilton Road Parson's Green SW6

Putney Bridge over the Thames River
Putney town is on the far bank of the river

Mrs Banks, Auntie Maude, Barbara and Brian

Kodak Baby Brownie

Selfridges in Oxford Street

My Baby Brownie camera that served me well for many years

Monday 27th October 1952: Today was terrible for me because I broke a couple of milling cutters. I was ashamed of myself as a tradesman, but sometimes these things happen. In my defence, the poorly lit machine was partly the cause, but primarily it was because I was back on piecework again, and was trying to hurry and gain a good bonus. It was a very traumatic day as my job at Bridges was in the balance. I was trying to hold on to it, although maybe it would have been better for me if they had sacked me. All was resolved when it was discovered that most of the milling cutters I was using to do the job, were blunt and needed sharpening, which was not my job. I should have been aware of this and refused to use them until they were sharpened. In the VR when milling cutters were returned to the store, they were immediately re-sharpened, so that the next user began work with a sharp cutter, but not here.

After dinner Ma Banks invited me to go to the motor show at Earl's Court with Barbara. "That would be great" I said. Before we went we had a beer and martini at the Railway Hotel in Putney, where I told them I had been to Earl's Court before, to see some of my work shown in an engineering exhibition. Earls Court Exhibition Centre is a large building with white rectangular columns and a semi-circular awning above the entrance.

The motor show exhibited mostly English cars, which negated some of the interest for me, but it was a good outing after the events of the day at Bridges. I wrote a letter to June Lucas, telling her I was looking forward to her arrival in London. However, I felt I must begin looking for a nice English girlfriend, but where to find one I wasn't quite sure.

Wednesday 29th October 1952: Surprise, surprise! I received a letter from Leon, saying he was leaving for Australia on the 29th of the month, today in fact. I think Leon was a Catholic, so the upcoming Coronation obviously did not mean as much to him as it did to me. I replied wishing him a safe voyage. Leon abandoned me in Bad Ischl, Austria on our first tour. To this day I do not know how Leon got on with his friends in Austria, after I saw his note in the Bad Aussie YH visitor's book. I knew he wanted to go to Vienna, but I did not see him there or his name in the Vienna YHA visitor's book. I am not sure too whether he worked in England or elsewhere. When I returned to Melbourne, I did not attempt to make contact with him, nor did he of me.

Thursday 30th October 1952: I saw a poster advertising *The Sound Barrier*, to be shown at the Putney cinema. I wanted to see the movie, especially after seeing Neville Duke on the TV earlier in the month, so I went along to the cinema. *The Sound Barrier* was an excellent movie, starring Ralph Richardson and Ann Todd. The film told the story of an aircraft manufacturer, that took risks with his friends and family, to prove that the sound barrier could be broken.

One of the great differences between going to the cinema in England and in Australia was that in English cinemas, smoking is permitted. In fact an ashtray is fitted into the back of every seat. Consequently one looked through a slight haze at the screen, which detracted somewhat from the enjoyment of the movie. I wondered too if I might suffer from someone in the seat behind me, discarding his cigarette butt or ash, down the collar of my shirt and not in the ashtray. In picture theatres in Australia, even though smoking is banned, there was always a fireman standing by on duty at the rear of the theatre, his axe at the ready, but ironically, there was not one to be seen in English cinemas.

Friday 31st October 1952: It was pay day again and not

surprisingly, considering the problems during the week, I only had an efficiency of 82 %, so there was no piece-work bonus for me. In the evening I watched TV and saw *Cafe du Paris* starring Diana Dors. My ideas of women and life were changing a little. I didn't consider myself to be a prude by any stretch of the imagination, but there were some things I saw on TV that made me cringe. Diana Dors the English sex sensation, belittled the beauty of the female sex and the boy-girl relationships, which I believe is a precious thing.

Chapter 5
DANCING AT THE PALAIS AND HARRODS

Saturday November 1st 1952; Reading my weekly copy of *Time* magazine, I discovered that the American presidential election campaign was in full swing. I also read a notice of a presidential election exhibition at the Pan-American Airline offices near Trafalgar Square, so I decided to go and have a look. The paraphernalia on display and for sale there was unbelievable; badges, flags, posters and much more. Truman had been the Democratic president since the last election in 1948, but he was not running for office this time. Dwight D. Eisenhower was the Republican nomination, opposed by the Democratic nominee Adlai Stevenson.

In the afternoon, I watched TV, until it stopped working. Mrs. Banks said she would get it fixed as soon as she could. Now that I was living in London I thought it was about time I contacted Mrs. Willshire, the lady my mother sent food parcels to during the war. I phoned her and she was thrilled to hear from me and said she looked forward to meeting me. I arranged to go to her house in Harrow on Sunday 9th November at 2 p.m.

Last week at work I heard a couple of blokes talking about dancing at the Hammersmith Palais. They said it was not far from where I lived. I decided to go and have a look. After dinner I got dressed in to my new suit, walked to Fulham Palace Road and caught the bus to Hammersmith Broadway and the Palais. The Palais is a large building with a huge dance floor. Ted Heath's band was playing at one end of the hall, while at the opposite end there was a long bar, the same layout as at the dance halls in Stevenage and Welwyn Garden City.

Most of the girls were on the young side and they were all chewing gum, which was not a pretty sight, certainly not my style. Even with free access to beer in the dance hall, I didn't see any evidence of drunkenness either inside or outside the hall. I must say again, that with English tap beer, one is full in the stomach-before one is 'full.'

The Ted Heath dance band was really fantastic. I just sat and soaked up the sound. I didn't even have a beer, nor sadly, did I see any girl I thought I might like to ask to have a dance. Saturday night dances at home were a weekly occasion when we dressed up in our best clothes, both boys and girls, but the standard of dressing was not as high at the Hammersmith Palais. There wasn't a bar in our dance halls either. I left about 10 p.m., deciding I would go again next Saturday night as I loved listening to the band, even though I didn't have a drink or dance.

Sunday 2nd November 1952: I rang Judy because she hadn't replied to the letter I sent her when I got back from my tour. She told me she was thinking of getting married, not to me of course, but to a bloke from the Brazilian embassy. I wished her well. Netta rang and invited me to go with her to the Lyric Hammersmith next Wednesday to see a stage play, *The Square Ring*. I said I would love to. Netta said she would get the tickets.

Tuesday 4th November 1952: It was good that the TV had been repaired because we were able to see all the news and celebrations from America about the election of their new President, Dwight. D. Eisenhower. I remembered that I had seen an A4, streamlined locomotive named after him, while watching the trains go by at Stevenage. He was indeed a famous general. A man I thought deserved to win the presidency.

Wednesday 5th November 1952: After dinner I picked up Netta and we went off to the Lyric Hammersmith an old cinema. *The Square Ring* was a good, earthy story about the boxing ring. During the show Netta pointed out the famous English actor John Mills, who was sitting just in front of us looking just as he does in the movies, rather ordinary. John Mills starred in many excellent English movies, *In Which We Serve* being one of his best, alongside Noel Coward.

When I returned from taking Netta home, I remembered that Wednesday 5th October was my younger brother, Donald's birthday. I'll have to send him a belated birthday card, very belated it would be in fact, by the time it reaches him. Friday pay day came around again, but I only had an efficiency of 81%. God knows how they worked it out. My pay was £6/11/3 (£7/10 gross). Good enough.

Saturday 8th November 1952: It was as a beautiful, cool, clear morning and everything looked clean and bright. I met Auntie Maude and Uncle Fred, Ma Banks' relatives at lunch. I then went with Uncle Fred to the Chelsea Football ground at Stamford Bridge. I had promised myself I would go and see an English soccer game, to satisfy my curiosity about the game the English call football, but we in Australia call soccer. From the soccer games I had seen previously in newsreels, I had to admit that the English game was football in the true sense of the word, much more so than our game of Aussie Rules. English football too, is a game played in nearly every country of the world, unlike ours.

Stamford Bridge is not far away from Chesilton Road. The ground is rectangular and not as big as Australian football grounds. Chelsea was playing Cardiff. Uncle Fred explained some of the finer points of the rules, such as the 'offside rule.' I told him all about Australian Rules and he said he would like to see a game. I enjoyed the novelty of watching my first live game of soccer, but was a little bored at times by the lack of action, with the players kicking backwards and forwards across the ground.

There is no comparison with the non-stop action of Australian Rules, as I told Uncle Fred. The unpredictable bounce of the Aussie Rules oval ball, also adds to the excitement of the game compared to the round ball. However, I enjoyed the game, and reckoned that if I were to follow a soccer team it would be Chelsea because of its proximity to Parson's Green, even though Cardiff beat Chelsea 2 nil. After the game we all went out to Gwyn and Sylvia's place at Wimbledon for dinner. There was no doubt that I was now accepted as a part of the greater Banks family, which was flattering and provided me with a sense of belonging.

After dinner I went again to the Hammersmith Palais. The band was the famous Victor Sylvester Dance Band, recognised as the leading, strict tempo, dance band in the world. I had danced to many of his records back home, so it was a great thrill for me to see and hear the band live. I had an enjoyable night this time, certainly a different experience from my first visit.

I danced with a pretty girl called Bernadette. In between dances, we talked about politics, religion and many other subjects. Bernadette was a Catholic. She gave me her phone number at the end of the night, so I added that to my collection, which was growing to enormous proportions, mainly due to having the use of

Ma Banks' phone.

Sunday 9th November 1952: I went with Ma Banks to Barbara's place for lunch. We had a couple of Guinness Stouts at a local pub beforehand, but I would never drink stout by choice, I don't like the taste. Barbara asked me if I would take her to a dance at Harrods on Wednesday 19th. Of course I said I would. Harrods the famous luxury department store. I couldn't believe I would ever get an invitation to dance there, but Barbara's sister Sylvia, who works at Harrods had given Barbara the tickets because she and Gwyn had another engagement.

After lunch I left Mrs. Banks with Barbara and went off to see Mrs. Willshire in Harrow. I caught a Piccadilly line tube train to South Harrow station, not very far from the Harrow and Wealdstone station, where the terrible accident occurred. From the station I walked a short way to the Willshire's semi-detached house, where I was greeted with outstretched arms by Mrs. Willshire, a middle aged, greying lady. She introduced me to her husband, a balding, pleasant faced man, then to the rest of her family two married sons and a single daughter. They were all so grateful to my mother for sending them food parcels, saying they were a marvellous help in difficult times. We had a great day together. I talked my head off because of course they all wanted to know about my family and my travels.

They asked me to stay for dinner and sat me down to a large delicious roast. I wondered if they had been saving ration tickets since the time I rang to say I was coming to visit them, so that they could put on a big meal for me. After dinner we wished each other goodbye and good luck. They asked if I would visit them again, but I didn't promise. I was too tired to write and tell my mother of my day at the Willshires. I would write a long letter tomorrow. My only regret was that I had not taken any photos of my family with me, or taken my new camera to take a photo of the Willshire family.

Tuesday 11th November 1952: I received a letter with photos of Heidelberg from my father. What a pity it was that I didn't have them when I was in Heidelberg Germany to show around. On the TV, I saw the excellent war documentary *Victory at Sea*. Then I wrote a very long letter to my parents about the Willshires. How wonderful it was to be with them and how thankful they were to receive the food parcels. I wrote about their family and the big meal they put on for me, and how it was really something special to meet these people. I had heard so much about the Willshires from my mother, sometimes posting the food parcels to them. I concluded the letter by telling my mother not to worry about me, as I had a job and board close by. Ma Banks my landlady was looking after me like a son, and I had become part of the greater Banks family. I brought them up to date with the happenings in Scotland, and how Heather was very sick. It was a very long letter with all the information about the Willshires and my news.

Thursday 13th November 1952: All the Banks family came to number 22 for the evening, Sylvia, Gwyn, and Barbara. I had a really enjoyable time with them all. It was obvious that Barbara was very lonely and missing her husband in Africa a lot. I hoped I would be able to cheer her up a little when I take her to Harrods's dance.

Friday 14th November 1952: I had a very pleasant pay day surprise. Bridges recorded my work efficiency as 181%, which earned me a pay packet of £12/5/7 (£10/6/10 after tax). It was the largest pay packet I had earned in England, including when I worked at Kings. It was still a puzzle to me however, how the system worked: I didn't think the work I did that week was any better than other, weeks when I only recorded a low efficiency. However, I wasn't going to argue, I would just take it and run.

Mrs. Banks and her friend Daphne were going to the movies and asked me if I would mind Daphne's two children, a girl aged 7 and a ten year old boy. I marvelled again at the family's trust in me, because that was the first time I had met Daphne. The children were no trouble at all, watching TV until they fell asleep in their chairs. That was the first time I had ever been a babysitter. I thought that maybe I should try and get a job as a nanny. Some of our Aussie nurses in London had great jobs as nannies through the agency, going to the Continent with rich people to look after their children.

Saturday 15th November 1952: I took my usual Saturday trip in to the West End, this time looking for a light blue jumper. I stopped at Harrods, but they were all too dear and not the style I wanted. After dinner I went to the Hammersmith Palais, where Ted Heath's Band was playing his wonderful music again. I had never seen so many gum chewing and characterless faces in my life at a dance hall,

I was sure that when Victor Sylvester's band was playing, the dancers who enjoyed dancing to his band were a different type to Ted Heath's followers. I danced with a girl from Finland named Zeeta, a student. She was very nice, so different. I took her home nearby and she gave me her phone number. My notebook is getting full of girls I am meeting, but none appear to be a short cut into the social life of London, or who I thought I would like to date.

Sunday 16th November 1952: I felt a little bored, so I rang Netta and asked her if she would like to come over and watch TV with Ma Banks and me. She did and we watched *The Merry Wives of*

Windsor enjoying the show, especially hearing one of my favourite tunes.

Monday 17th November 1952: I asked Ma Banks if she would like to meet a couple of Aussie nurses, and could I invite them over to watch the TV? She readily agreed. I rang Joan Cooper and Rosemary Roberts and asked them if they would like to come over and spend the evening with me and watch TV? "That would be lovely," they said. They were soon knocking on the door. After introductions to Ma Banks, we spent a most enjoyable night all four of us crowded around the TV, which they had only seen in shop windows. Ma Banks raved on to them, about what a beaut person I was. She said she loved meeting my Aussie friends, so I thought I must bring a few more around to meet her.

There were only two TV stations broadcasting in England. The first, and the third which commenced transmitting in 1947. The shows were excellent and generally to my taste. There was a great variety of programs, plays, comedy, opera, quiz contests and documentaries.

Wednesday 19th November 1952: After work and dinner I got myself ready to take Barbara to the Harrods's dance. It was raining like hell, so I took a taxi and picked up Barbara and a friend of hers. The dance was held in a large hall at the rear of the famous shop. Barbara was a good dancer and good company. I was not sure what sort of business it was, which kept her husband away for such long periods. Barbara was not a very happy person, and I suspected that the relationship between her and her husband was not the best. However, I think I managed to cheer her up a bit that night. There were a lot of lovely women at the dance and I wished I had been on the loose, because I thought there might have been an opportunity for me to meet someone who could get me an introduction into

London's social life. However I never let this thought get in the way of helping Barbara enjoy the night. At the end of the night, Barbara thanked me for a wonderful time and of course I thanked her for inviting me.

Thursday 20th November 1952: Gwyn and Sylvia were with us for dinner. Afterwards we played a hilarious game of Monopoly, then watched Sir John Barbirolli and the Halle Orchestra on TV. He appeared to be drunk, but I was told that he suffered from some complaint that makes him look that way. Gwyn and Sylvia thought he had asthma. I didn't know what the music was that was being played and that was a bit of a pity.

Friday 21st November 1952: I had a good efficiency this week, although by now, I had given up trying to determine how they worked it out. I also received a wage rise of 2 shillings per hour, thanks to the Amalgamated Engineering Union (AEU), but all those parasitic, non-union workers at Bridges and elsewhere in the UK received the rise as well. I paid my AEU membership fees for two years in advance before I left Australia, but sadly I found that very few workers in the UK belonged to a union. In some respects I believe, this accounted for the poor working conditions at Bridges, as there was no union to fight for any improvement. Good working conditions not only benefit the worker, they also benefit a company, as I believe they lead to a better quality product because employees are much happier and contented in their workplace, not to mention the safety aspect.

I have mentioned before how Australia lags behind the world in many aspects of life that I have observed while I have been abroad. There is no doubt however, that this is not so with regard to industrial working conditions in Australia, which are well ahead of those in the UK. The 40 hour week and fixed award wages for each trade, being just two of the conditions that Australian workers enjoy, most of which, particularly the 40 hour week, were gained only after a long campaign by the unions that involved many long strikes.

Saturday 22nd November 1952: I went to the Palais as usual on Saturday night, but nobody would dance with me. Most saying, "Sorry I don't dance." The Ted Heath band was the featured band again, so I just enjoyed the music and had a couple of beers before I went home. On the way out I had a word to the chap in the cloakroom. I said to him "Great dance hall this is, nobody would dance with me!" He looked at me and said "You don't look the type to enjoy it." Why, I wasn't sure. Maybe I thought, I should dress down a little, not wear my good suit and white shirt and perhaps chew a mouthful of gum. But no, I wasn't going to resort to that to get a dance.

Sunday 23rd November 1952: I slept in until 11 a.m. and in the afternoon I went to a skating rink in Richmond. It was only the second time I had been skating. The first time I went skating was at the Glacierium in Melbourne. I nearly killed myself because I tried to do on ice what I could do on snow on skis. It didn't work, and I fell heavily and nearly broke my skull. I knew this time to be very careful and I was, I had a good time without any bad falls, and I did learned one thing that afternoon, I would never be a skater!

Monday 24th November 1952: I rang up Netta and asked her if she would like to come over again and watch TV. Ma Banks was going out and we would have the TV to ourselves. As well as watching the TV we talked about many things, especially about the war in Korea, which had reached a stalemate. The future was going to depend a lot on the way President Eisenhower of the United States handled the situation. Being a retired general his ideas will be crucial. Neither of us saw much of the daily papers, most of which were tabloid. We thought *The Times* was the best. It was the one I had chosen to read in coffee bars in Vienna, and other places that had newspapers for customers to read. Netta and I thought that the tabloid newspapers were shameful. I remembered when I first arrived in England, *The News of the World* was doing an expose' of the Masons, handshake and all. After a pleasant evening with Netta I took her home to her flat in Clapham.

Years later I read that a well known, champion professional, English golfer (I believe it was Nick Faldo), had this to say about the British tabloid press. "It is the most vicious, cruel, ruthless entity on the face of this earth! It's difficult to express the depth of my contempt for them. They lie, fabricate stories and have an evil genius for exaggeration." These remarks are still true today as I write.

Tuesday 25th November 1952: I have been away from home for one year. My year away from home has really been an exciting learning experience. I had not really been homesick at all, because there was so much happening all the time, but I did get spasms of loneliness every now and again. However, they quickly evaporated as another exciting experience came along. It had certainly made me realise how very lucky we are in Australia. We don't know how well off we are.

Wednesday 26th November 1952: I invited Netta to come to the Hammersmith Palais with me and let her see what it was like on a Wednesday night. Even though Netta was in a bit of a complaining mood, she is a very good dancer as I discovered the nights we went to the *Rendezvous Club* in Grindelwald. Netta said she had a lovely time dancing with me to Ted Heath's band. I reckoned we were probably the best dressed couple on the dance floor.

Thursday 27th November 1952: Our Prime Minister, Robert Menzies was in London for the Commonwealth Conference. I saw his speech on TV and was shocked when I heard him speak, because I always considered he had a very English, upper class accent. Amazingly, he spoke with a real Aussie twang. I was of course living in an English environment with no regular contact with Australians, except for Netta and a few others from time to time. Whenever I heard an Aussie speak, the accent was immediately recognisable, and not all that attractive. In some ways very like the Cockney accent. After his speech I saw a shot of Collins Street Melbourne. It looked beaut with all the trees covered in leaves lining the street, because it was spring in Melbourne. In London at this time of the year the days are very short, it was nearly dark by about 4.30 p.m. The weather today was cold and sleety.

Friday 28th November 1952: Not only was it pay day, but also my regular bath night. The water was heated by a gas heater, which had to be fed with coins and there was no shower to be had afterwards. The London water supply was quite good, not at all like the bath water I had had to endure at the Bakers in Hitchin that left a thick watermark and really took some cleaning up afterwards.

Saturday 29th November 1952: It was too cold to go into London on Saturday morning, but as usual, I went to the Hammersmith Palais at night. I had a beaut night, meeting a vivacious girl Margaret Gadsden, who had a bit of a brain. It was the same surname as the girl who perished in the snow in 1943 on Mt Bogong, the highest mountain in my home state. I told Margaret the story, but she assured me there was no connection. I escorted her home and added her phone number to my list. She was one English girl I thought I would like to get to know better.

Sunday 30th September 1952: It was the last day of the month and the first day of autumn. I didn't wake up until noon and then went up to Barbara's house for dinner with Ma Banks. We made sure however, that we returned to number 22 in time to see the excellent TV show *What's My Line*.

Chapter 6
THE YOUNG CONSERVATIVE ASSOCIATION AND FOG

Monday 1st December 1952: After work today, while walking back to number 22, I saw an advertisement in a shop window, inviting young people to join the local Young Conservatives Association (YCA). Bingo! I thought this would be an ideal opportunity to meet young English people and maybe enter into the social life of London, and live the life of a 'Londoner'. I recalled that it was through the Conservative Party that I had entered the social life of Stevenage. I got a YCA membership application form from the shop that displayed the notice, which listed the time and place of the YCA meetings and the principles of the Association.

Reading carefully through it, there was nothing in the stated rules and principles that I disagreed with considering my union and Labor inclinations (Labor is spelt this way in Australia), so I decided to join. I had not formed any opinions about politics in Great Britain, except that I was rather saddened when I heard that the Conservative Party's Sir Winston Churchill had been defeated in the 1945 election by the Labour Party, after virtually winning the war for England.

The Labour Party that came after Churchill was led by Prime Minister Attlee and was responsible for many good social changes. I have them to thank for my new glasses and dental work, free of charge. Unbeknown to me at the time, Churchill and his conservative government were returned to power, earlier this year 1952. Mr. and Mrs. Baker, I thought, should be very happy now, although despite their complaining about the Labour Party, as far as I was concerned they had been doing an excellent job. It was the UK party I would normally have voted for.

Tuesday 2nd December 1952: The Young Conservatives met every Tuesday evening not far away from Chesilton Road. It so happened that this was the day after I found and read the advertisement, so I didn't have long to wait to find out all about YCA, and whether this would really be my entry into the social life of London. I went along and joined for the sum of 6 shillings and 6 pence (6/6) yearly subscription. There were about 15 young people at the meeting and I was welcomed and introduced to the members, who I thought averaged about 25 years of age, the same as me. Thank God none of them chewed gum. The meeting that night was a record and ear bash evening. At the end of the meeting, I was sure I was going to enjoy being a member of the club, and that was how I entered the exciting social life of London with the YCA.

Wednesday 3rd December 1952: I had a letter from Aleeta, my guide around the Heidelberg Castle thanking me for the photos of Heidelberg that I had asked my father to send to her. She wrote that she had shown them to a lot of people who were very interested to see Heidelberg in Australia, named after their home city. After dinner I rang Lionel and we went for a drink at the Star and Garter hotel, just across Putney bridge. Lionel told me all the latest YHA news. Especially of interest to me was that Lois, a blonde I dated back home, was engaged to Teddy Mohn and much more, all of which made me feel rather nostalgic. Teddy Mohn was a really nice bloke. I wished him luck, because I reckoned he would need it. As it turned out he didn't marry Lois, she dumped him just like she did me.

Saturday 6th December 1952: I went into the West End, which was enshrouded in thick fog, so much so, that I couldn't see one side of Piccadilly Circus from the other, although this did not seem to slow the buses down in the 'pea souper' fog at all. In the afternoon I had to put up with two squealing kids. Ma Banks was minding Brian and another child of a friend of hers for the weekend. They nearly sent me mad.

The fog in London in the morning was thick, but nothing like it was in the evening, when I decided get away from the kids and walk to the Star and Garter. Crossing Fulham Road, which is not a very wide road was a strange experience. I left the kerb on one side and with the opposite kerb invisible in the fog and darkness, it was quite weird. I just kept walking until the other kerb came into view. I managed to get to the Star and Garter, making my way along the path and cautiously crossing Putney bridge. The fog was so thick I couldn't see the surface of the Thames when I looked over and down the side of the bridge. I met a chap in the hotel from Bridges and we had a few drinks together. There was a dance on in the pub, so I had a few dances before deciding to return to number 22.

When I began walking back, a little the worse for wear in the thick fog, along the footpath over Putney bridge, to my surprise, just in front of me a car began to mount the kerb, its headlights virtually useless. I put my hand on the front mudguard and walked beside it guiding the driver to the other side of the bridge. That was how thick the fog was. I am not sure how he navigated his way to where he had to go after I left him. After that amazing experience, I noted as I had on the way to the pub that no buses were running along Fullham Road. The blinding fog was just too thick for them to continue running. I made my way back to number 22. The kids were still there so I went straight up to bed.

Sunday 7th December 1952; I woke up at 12 noon to find that both the fog and the kids were still with us. It was absolute bedlam! I tried playing with them, but they were too much for me, so without bothering to ring Netta, I went to see her in the afternoon to get away from them. The fog had cleared a little and the bus service had restarted. I climbed aboard the bus, which kept up a steady speed, not bothered by the fog at all. Arriving safely at Netta's flat, she introduced me to her friend Pam, a very lovely, young lady. I told them I had just joined the Young Conservatives, but they didn't seem that interested. We talked a lot about our experiences in the UK, and after having tea with them I went back to number 22.

Monday 8th December 1952: As I walked to work the fog had all but gone. The fog I had experienced during the past three days was the heaviest fog that London had ever experienced. It was referred to as 'The Great London Fog.' It was in fact more smog than fog, because whereas fogs are composed of condensed water vapour, this smog was a mixture of water condensate and smoke from the many, coal burning, household fires and factories, as well as exhaust gases from London's countless diesel buses and other vehicles. In Parson's Green and Putney, west of London, I found the fog to be fairly clean, as it had not soiled my white shirt too much on my Saturday night outing to the hotel. About the same as the collar of my white shirt would be soiled, after a day in London riding around in the tube.

Not so in the East End however, where the fog was very dirty indeed, due to large coal burning industries in that locality, as well as many more houses, all burning coal. I believe that everything was coated in a dirty black, sooty fallout, even invading the inside of houses. I thought it was ironic that the last electric London tram ran on 5th July of this year 1952, replaced by diesel buses. I actually never saw a tram in London, or knew about the closure. Due to breathing problems, the smog was responsible for many deaths, conservatively estimated at 1500 people according to newspaper reports. I also read that prize, stud bulls, at the Earl's Court cattle show were being 'fed' Johnny Walker Scotch whisky to help them breathe. How that helped I do not know. Later the Clean Air Act of 1956 imposed certain restrictions on coal burning, which helped to lessen the problem. There has never again been another fog in London, like the one I experienced in 1952.

I didn't see much of Mr. and Mrs. Cornish the other boarders at number 22. Mr. Cornish was a violin player in a small orchestra somewhere. I hadn't bought myself a radio yet, only the record player. I read that *The Beggars Opera* was going to be broadcast on the BBC Third Program and I didn't want to miss it. Talking to Mr. Cornish about my interest in *The Beggars Opera*, Mr. Cornish offered to lend me his radio, which I thankfully accepted. I took it up to my room and listened to the performance. The version of *The Beggar's Opera* I heard on the radio was the original English version, with words by John Gay and music by a Dr. Pepusch. It was sung in English, so I could understand most of what was being said and sung, somewhat different from the German version of the *Drei Groschen Oper*.

Tuesday 9th December 1952: I went to the YCA, where the subject for the night was 20 Questions, a quiz game, surprisingly without any overtones of politics. I wondered what the reaction of the members would have been if they knew I was a staunch, union supporter. I met a few more members of the club. I was just looking around, taking it all in to see what this association was really about, but so far it was beaut to be with them. It was especially encouraging when, at the conclusion of the meeting, Marjorie a lovely young lady asked me, "Will you be here next Tuesday?" She said the words in a manner that she hoped I would be, which gave me a good feeling. "Yes I will thank you." I replied.

Wednesday 10th December 1952: I got a long letter from my mother, telling me my father had deposited £50 into my bank account. Now I would be able to go home after the Coronation and please my mother, who I knew was missing me a lot. I wrote straight back to my parents thanking them for the loan. I really hadn't asked for one, but I may have hinted I might need one in one of my letters. Ma Banks bought a new grate for the fireplace in my room. She was really looking after me very well.

Saturday 13th December 1952: I went into the West End to the Orient Line booking offices. I told a booking officer, "My name is Gordon Smith and I have paid a deposit of £10 for a voyage on a P and O ship sailing sometime in August. Is there any information yet on upcoming voyages?" He looked up a folder and said "You are booked on the *Orion*, sailing on 18th September from Naples." I thanked him and he gave me a schedule of the voyage. I couldn't believe it when I saw that the date the *Orion* would arrive at Port Melbourne was my mother's birthday, 13th October! I thought it will be a wonderful birthday present for my mother, for her 51$^{st.}$

Then I went to Australia House, which I usually visited on Saturday mornings. Their noticeboards displayed all manner of information, newspapers too, all of interest to Australians living and passing through London. On this occasion I saw a notice that I hadn't seen before. There was to be an Aussie, Rules football match between crew members of the HMAS *Vengeance*, which was in port, in connection with a Commonwealth Conference to be held in London. The other team was being recruited through notices in Australia House. The match was to be played the next day, so of course I decided to go along.

On the way back to number 22 in the bus, I was trying to get my head used to the fact that I had actually booked a passage home. I now had to plan for the next nine months ahead, save money, see the sights of London and enjoy being a Londoner to the full. My tentative plan was to leave England a month before the sailing date, and make my way through Paris, then down to the French coast into Italy and finish up in Naples.

After dinner, I went to the Hammersmith Palais and had a fairly good night for a change. I had quite a few dances, although I didn't dress down. It was an old time dancing night, with the Victor Sylvester band. I came to the conclusion that the dancers who came when the Victor Sylvester band was playing, were totally different than when Ted Heath was the band. They were a little older, better dressed and didn't chew gum.

Sunday 14th December 1952: Gwyn and Sylvia were visiting Mrs. Banks for the afternoon. I decided to ask Gwyn if he would like to come and watch a game of Australian Rules football. He jumped at the opportunity, so off we went to Richmond Park. The standard of the game was quite high and it was good to see real, Australian Rules goal posts. Of course, the umpiring came in for a lot of abuse from the small crowd of spectators. Vengeance won 70 to 50 points.

Gwyn enjoyed the game and I tried as best I could, to explain some of the rules. He couldn't get over the speed of the game and the lack of an offside rule. I wondered if this was the first time, a properly organised game of Australian Rules football had been

49

played in the UK. I think it was. On the way home Gwyn told me they had just found out they were going to be parents in eight months time. That was great news for a beautiful couple. That night I wrote many Christmas cards to all my friends, to be posted the next morning.

In the 1980s at the end of the Australian football season, two Victorian teams came to the UK and played a demonstration game of Australian Rules football on the Oval. On one of these occasions the game developed into a big brawl. My team Essendon, was one of the teams that played and was involved in the brawl.

Tuesday 16th December 1952: I went to the YCA and met many new young people and heard a talk on the Borough Council, which was quite interesting. I was invited to a party on Saturday night and walked an attractive girl named Sylvia home. I also bought a ticket for the YCA Ball the following night. Sylvia already had a ticket. I offered to pick her up and take her there as she didn't live far away. She agreed. When I got back to my room I had a look at my dinner suit and decided it was OK to wear.

Wednesday 17th December 1952: After work I had a quick meal and dressed up to meet Sylvia at 8 p.m. Sylvia dressed for the ball in a lacy, black gown, just the thing for her lovely, slim figure and brown hair. I reckoned she was no older than 18. We took the bus to the Chelsea Town Hall where there were members from our YCA and other YCAs as well. It was a great night with a good band. They were a wonderful friendly group. I danced with a lot of different girls and had a few beers. Toward the end of the ball after I had danced with a number of other YCA girls, Sylvia attached herself firmly to me. I certainly didn't object. It was very nice to have an attractive, young girl, wanting to be with me.

After the ball we took a taxi home and finished up with a rather surprising, but exciting, deep kissing session in her front doorway. Before we parted, Sylvia asked me, "Would I take her out on Christmas Eve?" and I said, "I would love to." I finally climbed into bed at 3.30 a.m., after a wonderful initiation into the social life of London and an attractive new, rather hot, English girlfriend into the bargain. What could be better, I asked myself? At the same time I was a little wary of Sylvia.

Friday 19th December 1952: I came home after work to find letters from Bad Ischl and from May. May sent me a nice warm scarf and a beautiful photograph of herself, but it was sad to hear that Heather was still not getting any better. A letter also came from a YHA lady, Betty Nutting, telling me about the happenings in YHA. Netta rang and told me about a few more engagements of YHA members, some of which surprised me, others definitely not.

The YCA was having a night out at the Cafe Continental in Soho. After dinner I went by bus to the café, one of many coffee houses in Soho. Sylvia was there as well as some Australians from Sydney. I had a long and interesting talk with them about their plans abroad, which were to back pack around the UK and the Continent. They didn't know about youth hostels, so I told them about YH and my backpacking journeys. I had a good time at the Cafe Continental listening to records, drinking coffee, talking and dancing. At the end of the night Sylvia came over to me and without her having to ask, I took her home. I was finding it hard to resist her. She was just too lovely and desirable, a sexy young lady. Before Sylvia and I parted with many passionate kisses, she gave me a very attractive photo of herself and asked me to take her to a party the following night. How could I resist?

Saturday 20th December 1952: It rained in the afternoon and was very cold when I picked up Sylvia in the evening. I took a taxi with another couple of YCA members to a private house in Putney. I drank everything and met a stuck up girl from Harrow on the Hill, an 'Oh, I say-type.' Once again, it was an enjoyable night being involved in the young and exciting, social life of London with my newfound friends in YCA. I did not pay too much attention to Sylvia at the party because I was beginning to feel that she was a little young for me. Just a bit too attractive for my own good and hers as well for that matter.

After the party Sylvia and I began walking home together and had another kissing session in a shop doorway, which always seemed to be so convenient, but this time Sylvia wanted more. I being a normal young man, found her hard to resist. However, with great self control, I took the opportunity tell her that I felt that she was too young for me, and that I should stop seeing her. This led to a terrific discussion about ourselves in the shop doorway. I asked Sylvia how old she was and she said 17. I told her that if she was not careful she would get herself into a lot of trouble, and me too.

I escorted Sylvia home. With a final goodnight kiss, I hoped that was the end of it. I finally got to bed at 4.30 a.m. In the morning, Ma Banks said that she had waited up until 3 a.m. for me to come home. Perhaps I was mad with my worries about Sylvia. Why should I be worrying when I had a sexy, young girl who wanted to be with me and wanted to be loved? I asked a couple of male friends I had made at Bridges about the age of consent in the UK. They both assured me it was 16 years. I thought it would be wise to know, considering my involvement with Sylvia. I hoped however, that I had put an end to our relationship although I wasn't quite sure.

I have two mottos that I attempt to stick rigidly to. The motto of the MacRobertsons Girl's High School, *'Potens Sui'* (Master of

Self), or in other words, 'self control'. I learned this motto from the high school girls that I travelled with, and talked to in the train on my way home from work. The other, is the motto of the Scouts, *Be Prepared.* I have another of my own making. 'To know my limitations' that has kept me accident free skiing in Switzerland, and in my life.

Tuesday 23rd December 1952: Many Christmas cards were being delivered in the post from near and far, which was most encouraging. Ralph rang and told me he had a temporary practice in London and had bought himself a new car. That was great news. He invited me to come up to Stevenage with him next Saturday.

Tonight was a dance night at the YCA with music from a portable record player. Sylvia looked lovely, but I kept well away, but towards the end of the night she came over to me and reminded me that I had promised to take her out on Christmas Eve. I said "I will keep my promise."

Wednesday 24th December 1952: Christmas Eve. I worked until noon when everyone at Bridges got a £1 Christmas bonus. I then went to a pub with Syd, one of my friends from Bridges. We drank Trumen's Brown Ales and Scotch, a good combination. I was by now quite contented working for Bridges, despite the less than perfect working conditions and the dilapidated state of the machinery. My weekly pay was OK, sufficient for the lifestyle I was living as a Londoner.

After dinner I met Sylvia and we went into Trafalgar Square, where we admired the huge Christmas tree. Every year, the Norwegians send over a Christmas tree as a present to the people of London. It is erected in Trafalgar Square. For some reason, even though it was very dark on this Christmas Eve night, and although the tree was festooned with lights, they were not lit. This was a big disappointment for us both. I must admit it was great to have Sylvia's company as we walked around London hand in hand.

We went and looked at the Kon-Tiki exhibition, where I told Sylvia the story of the balsa raft, having read the book and seen *Kon-Tiki* in Norway. After Sylvia said she had seen enough, we went to a pub in Fulham Road, where we had a few drinks and began walking home, but detoured into a tennis court, where we indulged in a little 'love making' beside the clubhouse. The discussion we had had about our relationship a couple of nights earlier went out the window; because the truth was I couldn't resist her, but I must admit it warmed up the cold, Christmas Eve night.

I only wished that we could get together in my room, but I had to admit that Ma Banks's rule about not having any girls in my room, was a saviour for me, and of course my Potent Sui. I thought how fortunate I was to have a young girl like Sylvia, wanting to be close to me all the time, but it was also very frustrating. Later that night when I eventually took Sylvia home, I met her mother, Mrs. Elliot. She invited me to have a few Christmas drinks with them. I did and it was quite enjoyable, just the three of us downing a few beers. Mrs. Elliot was an attractive, pleasant natured lady, who didn't seem to have any qualms about her daughter being with me. I didn't know where Sylvia's father was and didn't ask.

Thursday 25th December 1952 I woke up late to a beautiful Christmas Day and later a tasty, Christmas dinner with all the family. I gave a present to Ma Banks and we played records on my player. I went out in the evening to a small YCA party, which was fun. Sylvia was there and after the party I took her straight home, with just a small goodnight kiss,. She asked me to promise to be with her on New Year's Eve. I said I couldn't promise, because I wasn't sure what my plans were. I didn't know how long Sylvia had been in YCA, but I am sure she just joined for the companionship. I felt sorry for her.

Friday 26th December 1952: Boxing Day is a holiday in Australia and the UK. After dinner with the family and Auntie Maude, I went to see Netta and her lot. Lionel was there and two, stuck up, Aussie women. They all went to the Old Vic, which left Lionel and me alone, so we rang up Joan Cooper and went out to see her.

Joan was working for a nursing agency and told us she was nursing King Hussein of Jordan, who had been struck down with a bad case of tonsillitis while he was training at the Sandhurst Army Training College. We smoked a couple of Hussie's (as they called King Hussein), gold tipped cigarettes he had left there when he visited the flat. Lionel left, leaving Joan and me alone.

Joan is a mature, attractive, happy brunette and qualified nurse. I had known her for a long time in YHA, as one of the YHA Buller mob. We got on very well together and although there was a good feeling between us, I never dated Joan back in Australia. I bought some Dress Gordon tartan material and Joan offered to make it into a shirt for me. This I think brought us closer together. We met a number of times in London and last October. I took Joan out for the day and we had a lovely time together. We vowed to go out on a date again, but with everything that was going on in my life, this was the first time since then that we had really been alone together.

After sitting on the couch for a while and talking small talk, we put out the light and pleasured each other with harmless, love making until 2 a.m. It happened quite spontaneously because of the mutual attraction we had for each other over many years. So different from young Sylvia's sexual desires. I think Sylvia was a lonely, young lady and above all, craved companionship. All of this love making with Sylvia and Joan, although, delightful and exciting, was very frustrating. I reckoned I must be the most frustrated man in London and me, with my inferiority complex, that Netta says I have.

Saturday 27th December 1952: I rose at noon and went into the West End. I took a photo of the still, unlit Christmas tree in Trafalgar Square. Then to King's Cross station, where I caught the train to Hitchin in thick fog. Ralph was at the station to meet me with his brand new car, a black, Ford Consul, his wife Gladys, Brian and Sheila. Jim and Jean were somewhere else. We went back to Sheila's for a restful afternoon. In the evening we all went to a charity concert, which was really horrible. I slept at Sheila and Brian's place.

Sunday 28th December 1952: Jean and Jim arrived and all the men went to the Crooked Billet a quaint, old pub, close by. We had a few ales there and played darts before returning to Sheila and Brian's house, where we sat down to a succulent, roast lunch prepared by Sheila and Jean. I returned to London with Ralph and Gladys in the new Consul arriving at number 22 in the dark, after a very pleasant couple of days with my old friends. Ralph was allowed to drive his car with his New South Wales license for two months, after that he would have to get an English licence. Ralph and Gladys were living apart and when Ralph had a few drinks, he became very sad and many times he said to me. "You can have her mate, take her." Of course I did not entertain any such thoughts, even though Gladys lived close by in London and Ralph had given me her address and phone number.

Monday 29th December 1952: Among the many letters that I received, was one from Auntie Ruby telling me that Heather had

The unlit Christmas tree in Trafalgar Square

Sylvia my femme fatale

Aussie Rules football at Richmond Park arranged by Australia House

A photo of the Kon TiKi from the museum

YCA group at the ball the author is second from the left

King Hussein (elect) of Jordan

passed away. It was very sad and I felt for the family in Scotland. Heather's death was the result of hepatitis, which is now curable. Heather was a lovely, but frail, young girl who I never really got to know in the short time I was there. Although the family realised it was inevitable, the loss would have been a great blow to them all, especially because it occurred between Christmas and the New Year. I could only hope that she had passed away quietly, without pain.

Tuesday 30th December 1952: I selected an appropriately worded condolence cards and sent them to Uncle John, Auntie Greta and May, together with a letter telling them of my sorrow at the news. I wrote a similar letter to Uncle Bob and Auntie Ruby. Although I was sure they would be writing to my mother, I also wrote to tell her the sad news.

Tonight at the YCA we danced to records, talked and enjoyed ourselves, nothing special. At the close of the meeting Sylvia asked me to take her home, take her out, ring her and spend her birthday with her. Where was her father I wondered? I walked Sylvia home but made no promise to ring or take her out. We bade each other goodnight with a simple kiss and hug, but nothing more.

Chapter 7
THE NEW YEAR AND BEING STOOD UP FOR A KING

Thursday 1st January 1953: I had already purchased a 1953 diary, about the same size as my very worn 1952 diary. The 1952 diary had two days on each page whereas my new 1953 diary only has one. This meant that my 1953 entries would not need to be so cryptic. It would allow me more space to enter the events and thoughts of each day, without the need for as many supplementary notes. After bringing the New Year in at the Railway pub in Putney with Ma Banks and Barbara, we went to Barbara's for a cup of coffee, then in the early hours of the morning Ma Banks and I went back home on the bus. I had only made one New Year's resolution. To be happy and stay out of trouble, especially with Sylvia.

Unlike Australia, New Year's Day in the UK, is not a holiday, so off to work I went with little sleep, a hangover and a bad cold. The English I thought are really uncivilized, workers like me, having to go to work with a hangover, how unproductive and dangerous is that? My nose ran all day, but I managed to last until knock off time, completely buggered. Back home after dinner I was heading off to bed, when Ralph rang up Ma Banks and asked if she could put him up for two weeks from Sunday 11th of this month? He told her he would be leaving his dental practice in Hitchin and looking for another in the country. Without consulting me, Ma

Banks told him it would be OK if he bunked in with me in the double bed.

Friday 2nd January 1952: I woke up late and when I went down to have my breakfast, Ma told me of the arrangement she had made with Ralph. I wasn't very pleased. I told Ma Banks, I certainly wouldn't be happy if I had to share my double bed with Ralph. He was a great bloke and a wonderful friend. I would be very happy if we could fit him in at number 22, but not in my bed. I told Ma Banks that as good a friend that Ralph is. The best in fact, it was a definite 'no-no'.

Saturday 3rd January 1952: Ma Banks must have phoned Barbara, because the next day Ma told me that Barbara had offered to take him in for the two weeks. Problem solved.

Monday 5th January 1953: When I arrived home from work, there was a great bundle of the *Argus Weekend Magazines* in the mail from my parents. This was an excellent supplement to *The Argus*, a Melbourne daily newspaper, a cross between a tabloid and a broadsheet paper. Sadly *The Argus* became defunct a year or so after I got back to Australia. The copies of the *Argus Weekend Magazine* provided me with many hours of interesting reading. Ma Banks and the other members of the family also found them of great interest. I wrote to Tom Webb and June Lucas at her forwarding address, because I didn't know where she was. Last but not least, I wrote to my parents to thank them for the magazines. I spent some of the evening watching TV with Ma. We saw our test cricketers and then *Victory at Sea*.

Tuesday 6th January 1953: I received a letter from the Danish girl Helle, asking me why I had not phoned her? I should never have promised to take her out, so I made another New Year resolution. 'Don't make promises'. There was also a letter from

May, which I replied to that night. At the YCA meeting Sylvia was there, but I kept my distance virtually ignoring her, although I was not sure if that was the correct attitude. Time would tell. I wrote to Helle saying that I could not take her out at present.

Wednesday 7th January 1953: It had been snowing a little the last two days and now it had iced up. The cars driving along Fulham Road had to be very careful. It had stopped snowing, but it was bloody cold, especially at Bridges where there was no heating provided for the workers; we just had to rug up. After dinner I visited Netta. Nellie was there with her daughter. We had an interesting conversation about all sorts of subjects. Nella's daughter who I felt disliked me, seemed to have got over that. I told them all about my life with Mrs. Banks and how I was considered to be one of the family. Nellie warned me not to let Mrs. Banks become too much of a tie. I said that I appreciated their acceptance of me because it gave me a sense of belonging and a sense of being a Londoner.

Friday 9th January 1953: I was glad that I had stuck it out working at Bridges, because I had got used the inconvenient working conditions and the piece-work pay was nearly as much as at Kings, sometimes more. My workmates were OK and even though the condition of the machines was poor I had become used to their various quirks, which meant I was able to turn out a good job, enabling me to earn acceptable bonuses.

At last, I saw a new machine at Bridges. A new copying lathe had just been installed. It was a new concept in machine tools and was made in Switzerland. It was being used at Bridges to turn metal or wooden handles and other components, normally turned in manually operated lathes. It was basically a standard lathe except that it worked automatically, by copying a sample component mounted on the lathe. A stylus moving slowly along the sample, traced the shape of its contours. The movements of the stylus were translated by an electro-hydraulic control system, imparting a corresponding movement to the lathe tool. This action cut the spinning work piece, making an exact replica of the sample component. All the operator was required to do was to remove the finished product, insert a new work piece and restart the machine.

I relaxed in the evening and on the TV, watched *Kaleidoscope* and *What's My Line?* BBC TV did not give cash prizes for any of its quiz shows. I rang Joan Cooper and asked if she would like to go 'pub crawling' tomorrow night. She said she would love to, so I arranged a time to pick her up. Ma Banks, like Mrs. Baker in Hitchin, was Conservative mad. I was really in her good books after I joined the YCA. That evening we had a good discussion on politics and she told me a little about her life. Her husband was killed in the war. It seemed she had been through quite a lot, but was doing an excellent job as a landlady.

Saturday 10th January 1953: When I went into the West End, I saw workmen beginning to put up the stands for the Coronation in Green Park. So soon I thought, but it would set the scene for the big event in five months time. It was quite exciting to see. I wondered where along the route of the procession, I would be sitting in a grandstand. Then I went to the bank in Berkeley Square where I found I had 37 Aus. (£28 Sterling) in my account. I thought this was not too bad and should grow steadily, because I was saving about £1 a week. Dad's £50 was in a separate account.

Joan rang in the afternoon to tell me she was sorry, but our 'pub crawl' was off. She was going out with the King of Jordan instead! He was taking her for a flight over London, so I certainly couldn't compete with that. I was stood up again. This time in favour of a

King. That I thought, was really something to write home about. Joan said she would ring me tomorrow. I wished her a good flight.

King Hussein (Husayn) was born in 1935 in Jordan, the son of Crown Prince Talal. While accompanying his grandfather, King Abdullah on a journey in 1951, he witnessed the assassination of his grandfather, the King. Talal became King, but due to a medical condition abdicated after only two months. Hussein became the Crown Prince of Jordan (King elect) at the age of 16, but could not assume the title of King, until he turned 18 in 1953. In the meantime he studied in England at Harrow. In 1952, he joined the Royal Military Academy at Sandhurst as an officer cadet. During his training at Sandhurst he contracted acute tonsillitis, and this was how Joan Cooper came to be involved with him. Joan was assigned through the nursing agency to nurse Hussein, whom she referred to as 'Hussey', but of course, not in his presence.

When Hussein became King of Jordan in 1953, Joan received an invitation to the coronation, but did not attend. King Hussein was a very popular King, with a young outlook on life. He was pro-western in his dealings and thoughts, even to the extent of marrying an English girl Toni Gardiner, after his divorce from his first wife. Toni was given the title of Princess Muna and bore him two sons and two daughters. Sadly, Hussein died at the relatively young age of 70 years. This was the man I had the honour of being stood up for, and I hoped it would be the glorious end of my record of being stood up so many times!

I went to see Netta and told her what had happened with my date with Joan. She thought it was a huge joke; so did I actually. Netta didn't want to go on a 'pub crawl,' so instead we went to see *The Man Who Watched the Trains Go By,* starring Claude Raines and Herbert Lom. It was a very good film.

Monday 12th January 1953: After I came home from work, Ma and I had the following remarkable conversation around the dinner table.

"Ma, I see the *Daily Graphic* has changed its name to the *Daily Sketch* and I believe it supports Labour."

"Oh, does it? I didn't know. I will cancel it then."

"But Ma, you have got to read both sides."

"Oh no, I will cancel it!"

But she didn't. I thought to myself, what hope does one have with this form of thinking. The pity of it is that so many people do not think and vote on the real issues, but on a party, most times influenced only by hereditary. My father was a Liberal voter. We had many arguments, because after I commenced work, my ideas of justice and fair play were aligned to the Labor Party. I admired Prime Minister Menzies, the leader of the Liberal Party, at least for his support of the Crown.

Joan Cooper rang and told me that she had had a great time flying over London with King Hussein, and that June Lucas would be arriving in London at St Pancras Railway Station at 3.30 p.m. the next day. If I wanted to see her, I would have to leave work early, so I decided to do just that.

Tuesday 13th January 1953: I left work at 3 p.m. and made my way to St. Pancras. There was quite a welcoming party to meet June on the station, Joan Cooper, Rosemary Roberts, as well as Mrs. Lucas, June's mother, who I had met many times before in Australia, when taking June home from a date. June and her mother both sailed on the same ship to the UK. June left the ship in Naples, but Mrs. Lucas stayed on and was here to greet her daughter. We all waited with baited breath until at last the train pulled in.

June came towards us along the platform with a girlfriend, who she introduced to us all, by the curious name of 'Podge.' Podge was plump but pretty, in stark contrast to June, who looked lean and haggard after their tour of the Continent. We all had a cup of tea on the station. I told June how I had left my rucksack on Waterloo Station, as a reminder to make sure she didn't leave anything behind on St Pancras Station. June would be boarding in the flat with Joan, Rosemary, and the other nurses. I left it in June's hands to contact me.

Chapter 8
TOURING AROUND ENGLAND IN RALPH'S NEW CAR

Wednesday 14th January 1953: After work Ralph came to see me. He had just moved into Barbara's place for two weeks while he looked for a new dental practice. I hoped young Brian didn't drive him mad, but as a dentist he should be able to handle young kids. Ralph asked me if I would like to go with him the next day to Dover? He said he wanted to have a look at a couple of dental practices. It meant that I would miss a day's work, but it would be good to see more of England, so I readily agreed.

Thursday 15th January 1953: I was up early, looking forward very much to the drive, but first I rang Bridges to tell them I would be away for the day. There was a touch of fog around as Ralph picked me up and we drove out of central London. The fog had lifted and it was a nice sunny day as we drove through Kent towards Dover. Ralph said we would share the driving. Both Ralph and I were relatively inexperienced drivers. With Ralph driving and me navigating, we left the London traffic behind and were on the A20 highway with 125 km to go, before we reached Dover. The Ford Consul was motoring along beautifully, until somewhere between Maidstone and Ashford, we came to a spluttering stop!

Before this happened, we had been commenting on the actions of the Automobile Association (AA) and the Royal Automobile

Club, (RAC), motor bike and sidecar patrolmen. As they passed us going in the opposite direction, we were always given a salute, even though we were not carrying either the AA or RAC emblems, such was the road customs at the time. Quite perplexed with our breakdown, we got out of the car, opened up the bonnet and tried to find out the reason for our sudden stop. We had filled up with petrol just out of London, so it was not a case of running out of petrol (or so we thought). We were still looking at the engine and it could not have been more than five minutes, before an AA patrolman pulled up alongside our car, saluted and said, "Can I help you, sir?"

Ralph replied, "Mate, we are not members of the AA."

"That's all right sir, here is an application form you can fill in, while I attend to your car."

In no time at all the patrolman found the problem, which was a blocked petrol filter. He told us that this was a common fault with new cars, as some dirt managed to get into the petrol lines during manufacture. Ralph wrote out a cheque there and then, and became a member of the AA. I suspected that once he got the badge fitted to his car, he would only be saluted to by an AA patrolman in future.

I took over the driving through the beautiful, rolling countryside of Kent until we reached Dover. That was really the first time I had travelled by car on a long drive through the English countryside, previously it had always been by coach or train. It was especially beaut to be driving a new car, after my brother Donald's old Vauxhall. There is no doubt that the English countryside is lovely, even with the trees stripped of their leaves and a little snow on the ground here and there. I was amused at the delightfully, peculiar names of some of the villages we passed. Names such as Little

Chart, Ram Lane, Bapchild and others. They appeared to be silly names, but no doubt there were valid reasons for being so called.

When we arrived in Dover, Ralph had a look at two practices, but wasn't very impressed with either. We had lunch and walked around Dover with its large docks. We of course saw the white cliffs of Dover, which really are white, so white, that I reckoned they must hire someone to whitewash them every now and again. I had not been to Dover before; because when I crossed the Channel, it was always Folkstone Harbour that I left from and returned to.

On the way home we took the road to Canterbury. The town was badly damaged by bombing during the war, but there was very little damage to be seen now. Canterbury lay right on the path of the German bombers as they crossed the English Channel on their way to London. If they had any bombs left on their way back to Germany, it was in this area that they dumped them.

Canterbury with its cathedral is a very historic town. It is the residence of the head of the Anglican Church, the Archbishop of Canterbury. Canterbury Cathedral (Christchurch) is basically a Gothic style church, in the form of a cross with the transepts forming the arms of the cross. These, however, were not very significant because the cathedral had chapels built onto both sides, which tended to disguise the transepts.

We inspected the cathedral and saw where Thomas A'Becket was murdered, and the tombs of the Black Prince and King Henry IV. We admired the cathedral's beautiful stained glass windows, which were removed during the war to prevent them from being damaged. The building of the church began in 1070, although the foundation was laid much earlier. During construction over the centuries, the church was destroyed by fire on a number of occasions. It also went through a number of design changes, even up to 1832, when the last of the additions and alterations were made. This resulted in the cathedral that we saw being grand, but to my mind, not beautiful. As is my wont for likening a church to a mountain, regrettably I could not think of any mountain that had some similar characteristics to Canterbury Cathedral. Leaving Canterbury, we drove back to number 22 through the darkening day. I bade goodbye to Ralph, thanking him for a very enjoyable day of driving and sightseeing.

Friday 16th January 1953: Back to work and home to a beaut bath and a nice meal of sausages and mashed potatoes. On Friday nights when I had my weekly bath, Ma supervised me to make sure I didn't waste the gas and make the water too hot, and then having to cool it down. I well-remembered the first time when I put the bath water on. Ma Banks saw steam rising from the water in the bath and she said, "It's hot enough now."

"Ma, steam can be seen to rise from an ice cold lake." I replied.

Ma Banks often served me up sausages and mash, sometimes saying, "Nice for a change." They were nice, but not much of a change. I couldn't complain, because I had never left her table feeling hungry, and that was a great compliment to her.

After dinner I relaxed and watched the delightful opera *Hansel and Gretel* by the German composer Humperdinck. *Hansel and Gretel* is a children's fairy tale opera, which has some delightful tunes and songs, a couple of which I decided I must get on record. The part of Hansel is usually sung by a mezzo-soprano, as it was in this production. The two singers were Gertrude Holt and Marion Studholm. *Hansel and Gretel* I thought was a wonderful opera for a young person to see, for their first experience of opera going. With arts such as ballet and classical music, I believe a young person's first experience, should be carefully selected to ensure that the performance provides a happy and interesting occasion. For a young person's first ballet, I would suggest *The Nutcracker*.

As for classical music, there is so much to choose from. The first concert I went to was with the Boy Scouts in the Melbourne Town Hall. The work I heard and was captivated by was, Tchaikovsky's *5th Symphony,* maybe a little heavy, but it did me no harm. Otherwise, Berlioz's *Fantastic Symphony* would be an excellent choice too, especially if the listener knows the story of each movement of the symphony.

Saturday 17th January 1953: I went into London and updated my driving licence at the AA offices, then got a ticket to see the musical *Porgy and Bess,* playing at the Stoll Theatre in Kingsway. *Porgy and Bess* is an American musical about the Negro goings on in Catfish Row and a crippled beggar, who cares for a beautiful girl. I liked some of the songs, 'I Got Plenty O' Nuttin', 'Bess You Is My Woman Now' and the lullaby 'Summertime.' I went by myself and enjoyed my company very much. I thought the show was OK but nothing special.

Sunday 18th January 1953: I rang Netta to see how she was going. She invited me to come for tea with Nellie and her flat mates. All of Netta's flat mates and Nellie are Catholics. After a nice meal, I became embroiled in an enthralling discussion on religion. I contributed to the discussion, by explaining how I was brought up as a Baptist, attending Bible classes until I was 21. However, I failed at being a Baptist; because the belief that Jesus rose from the dead was beyond my powers of logical reasoning.

I believe, that some of the Ten Commandments are very good tenets, but the Boy Scout's tenets: 'trusty, loyal and helpful, brotherly, courteous, kind, obedient, smiling, thrifty, pure as the rustling wind,' are the ones I try to live by. There was an unofficial addition to these. 'A scout is not a fool.' I said that the early history of Catholicism was nothing much to be proud of, nor were the actions of the Pope's very Christian, during the last war with respect to the Jews, a statement that nobody there disagreed with, I was pleased to say.

Monday 19th January 1953: Ralph came round in the evening just as the BBC was repeating *Hansel and Gretel*, so we all watched it together. Ralph wanted to go to the Midlands to look at more dental practices and asked me if I would like to come along? Of course I said yes. I noticed later, that there was an ominous fog warning on the TV for the next day.

Tuesday 20th January 1953: I rang Bridges to tell them I would be away for a couple of days. Sure enough, it was quite foggy when Ralph picked me up, but as soon as we got to Harrow on the Hill in the north of London the fog disappeared. In its place we beheld a beautiful, crisp, frosty, and cloudless day. We drove along the A5, passing through Luton and Milton Keynes in Buckinghamshire.

Even considering the lack of flowers in bloom and that most of the trees were bereft of leaves, the English countryside in the depths of winter, has a charm of its own. This is especially so with a slight mist covering the fields, and the sky above showing just a bare trace of light blue. It was just under 200 km to Birmingham, England's second largest city, and our first destination in the West Midlands.

We bypassed the large city of Coventry and reached Birmingham in time for a late lunch. Birmingham's large industrial centre was heavily bombed by the Germans. There was still much bomb damage to be seen, but there was also a lot of building taking place. After lunch, while Ralph took some time looking at a dental practice, I relaxed and read a book in the car and watched the passing parade of cars, buses and people.

Leaving Birmingham, our next destination was Nottingham of Robin Hood fame, 80 km distant in Nottinghamshire. The days were still very short and it was soon dark. I was driving and had to admit, I was a little scared at the new experience of night driving. We eventually stopped at a little town called Ashby-de-la-Zouch in Leicestershire, and booked into a hotel.

The county of Nottinghamshire is the home of Worthington beer, reputedly a good drop, which the hotel had on tap. There was nothing else to do, so we both got stuck into a few beers to see if what was said about the beer was true. It was and surprisingly, we managed to get very full alcoholically, before we were physically full in the stomach, quite an achievement for an English beer, I thought. Ralph told me I had lots of potential, which was a nice change from Netta telling me I had an inferiority complex, but probably it was the beer talking.

Wednesday 21st January 1953: It was quite a task for us to get out of bed the next morning. When we paid our bill, the proprietor asked us if we were going to visit the famous castle. We hadn't noticed any castle when we drove into the town in the dark, but we decided we would have a look. We drove down the road where he directed us and discovered there was a guided tour of the ruined castle and the abbey at the rear of the town. We of course decided to join the tour.

The guide informed us that Ashby-de-la-Zouch was named after a Norman family who built the castle in 1461. It was later turned into a fortress. The castle was used to imprison Mary Queen of Scots in 1569. It was also featured in Sir Walter Scott's novel *Ivanhoe*, which I had read at school, but I couldn't remember much about it. Ashby-de-la-Zouch was also the home of Lord Byron.

The guide asked if we had heard the 1947 hit tune written about the town and castle, sung by the Merry Macks? When he hummed a bit of the tune, we both recalled we knew it very well when it was on the hit parade. We at once remembered that although the words, 'Ashby-de-la-Zouch by the sea' are repeated a number of times in the lyrics—in fact, Ashby-de-la-Zouch is 120 km from the sea. Nevertheless it is a lovely song and tune. The guide never mentioned, nor did we ask the reason for this enigma. It was a very interesting diversion for Ralph and me to see the castle and its history, and its connection to the song.

There's a village that I love in Leicestershire
Always had my heart enthralled
Where the stars are bright above in Leicestershire
Believe or not it's called
Ashby de la Zouch, Castle Abbey
That's the only place that I long to be,
Skies are full of blue, and the cows are full of moo
In Ashby de la Zouch by the sea
Ashby de la Zouch, Castle Abbey
It's a little bit of heaven for me
Girls have pretty curls, and the boys have pretty girls
In Ashby de la Zouch by the sea

Leaving the castle the weather was still quite pleasant as we drove north west through the beautiful, rolling countryside, toward Nottingham. When we arrived there we had lunch. As usual, I stayed in the car while Ralph inspected a couple of practices. I liked the look of the wide, open industrial city of Nottingham, famous for the adventures of Robin Hood and his merry men, in the forest of Sherwood, located 28 km north of the city. The Players Cigarette Company factory is in Nottingham, so I bought a packet of Players to assist the city's economy and had a cigarette or two while I waited for Ralph.

Strangely, I didn't see any bomb damage in Nottingham, such as I had seen in Birmingham. The Germans must have considered that Birmingham was a much more important industrial target, even though Nottingham was a centre for various large industries. They must have saved their bomb loads for Birmingham and Coventry, which they blasted to hell. This may have saved Nottingham. I would have liked to have dallied a while around Nottingham and explored the city and its environs, but we had to move on.

As soon as Ralph was ready, we made a start on the 194 km journey back to London along the A606. I was driving. Not far out of Nottingham, I had a frightening incident on the highway. I pulled out to pass a truck, where I thought there was ample visibility ahead, but when I was about halfway along the length of the truck, I saw a car coming toward me at what appeared to be a very fast pace. Unfortunately, I cut back to my side of the road a little too early and just scraped the truck as I passed. "No problem," Ralph assured me."

Looking back on the incident a short while later, I realised that there was plenty of room to pass safely, but being a new and inexperienced driver, I had panicked. The scratch was very minor and I was glad when Ralph took over soon after. It quickly became dark as we drove the rest of the way back to London.

The main roads I was used to back home in Victoria were asphalt surfaces bordered on both sides by gravel, about a car's width wide. If for any reason a car needed to leave the asphalt surface to park or otherwise, it was only necessary to slow down and pull over to the side. This manoeuvre was only dangerous if the gravel surface was soft, or the driver braked suddenly. Most of the main roads that we had been driving on during the past two days had defined borders on both sides of the asphalt surface. They consisted of a raised concrete strip, about 75 mm wide, protruding about 50 mm above the road surface. If a car had reason to leave the road surface, it first had to mount and cross this border strip, which looked a little hazardous.

Ralph and I had commented on this characteristic of English main roads compared to those back home. I think that subconsciously, I had those raised border edges in my mind, and imagined that the approaching car could not easily leave the asphalt to get out of my way. Without any further problems on the road, we reached number 22 just in time for dinner, which Ma put on for us both. After dinner I said goodnight to Ralph and thanked him for the great two days on the road, and apologised for putting a dent in his new car. He said not to worry about it and thanked me for helping him in his search for a new practice, although none of the ones he inspected were suitable for his needs.

Before getting into bed I wrote up my diary and notes for the last two days, as it had been all a bit too hectic to write them up each night, because on one of those nights I was incapable of writing anything! Ralph and I talked a lot about ourselves on this trip. Ralph was a very good friend and confidant. He wanted to get out of his marriage with Gladys. He had been urging me to give him a cause. Although Gladys was a very attractive woman, I was not interested in her in any way, nor had she shown any interest in me. I was gradually learning a lot about the opposite sex. I kept my distance from Gladys, although Ralph wished it was otherwise. I didn't think I would have been able to afford Gladys, but I would very much have liked to see Ralph free of her, without any complications.

Chapter 9
AN EXCITING WEEKEND IN STEVENAGE

Friday 23rd January 1953: Pay day again. I had an excellent efficiency of 132%, but as this was only for three days work, so my pay was small. After dinner Ralph picked me up in the car. We drove up the Great North Road to The Unicorn pub in Stevenage where we met the mob. We had a few drinks with Brian and Sheila, Thelma and Neil, friends of Sheila and Brian that I hadn't met before. Then it was off to a police dance. I was disappointed Marie wasn't at the dance, because I would have liked to see her again.

Going to bed at Sheila's at 3.30 a.m. reinforced my stand about not wanting to share my bed with Ralph, or any male for that matter. On this occasion, Ralph and I shared a double bed at Sheilas. During the night, Ralph must have thought I was Gladys. He was talking in his sleep, saying. "Gladdy, Gladdy" and trying to hug me. I pushed him off and managed to convince him that I certainly wasn't Gladys!

At the breakfast table, I asked Brian if he had a 6 by 4 board to put between Ralph and me in the double bed. They all looked puzzled at me until I explained what had happened during the night. They thought it was hilarious, although Ralph poor bugger, was very embarrassed.

"Did I do that? I'm very sorry mate," he said.

Of course we were all very sorry that Ralph and Gladys had broken up and told him we all understood. As I had intended it was all joked away.

Jean and Jim came around for dinner, a succulent meal of roast pork, then we all drove down to a dance at the Cherry Tree in Welwyn Garden City. Once again it was a pleasure dancing at this large hall and having a drink or two between dances. As if my near accident coming back from Nottingham wasn't a big enough scare, coming home from the dance along the Great North Road, I had another big scare, this time in the back seat of Jim's Morris Oxford. It was hair-raising experience! Jim was driving extremely fast, despite a heavy fog. He was just using the cat's eyes in the centre of the road for guidance. Lucky for us there were only a few cars coming in the opposite direction and most were going slowly. Thankfully he managed to move over as they passed by.

Sunday 25th January 1953: I helped Brian in the hothouses tending to the lovely, large marrows, then we went and had a drink at the Crooked Billet where we played an interesting game of cricket on the dart board. After that, it was off to Jean and Jim's house in Hitchin for a beaut lunch. We drove back to Sheila's very slowly, because we had all had, quite a bit to drink. The activities of the mob were not finished yet, because in the evening we went up to the Brewhouse Inn.

It was great to be there again after such a long time. It is one of the most congenial pubs I had visited in England. After a few games of darts and only one beer for Ralph, we set off for London. The exciting events of the weekend were not yet over yet; because we ran out of petrol in the suburbs of London, and had to push the Consul to the nearest service station. That was the sort of weekend it was. I arrived back at number 22, dog tired, but more to the point bloody broke.

Monday 26th January 1953: Back to work, but very tired. After work I told Ma I am having my friends from Stevenage down on Sunday. She said that would be alright as long as there was no drinking in the room. I assured her that there wouldn't be. I asked her if it would it be OK if they had a quick look at the TV, because they didn't have it up where they live? Yes she said, so it was all arranged. We told Ma Banks we would be going to the Star and Garter afterwards.

Tuesday 27th January 1953: I went to the YCA and asked Sylvia if I could take her home. We finished up with only a good night kiss, but no arrangement to see each other again. I had been having some thoughts about Sylvia. I was feeling that I might have been a bit harsh, hence my asking to take her home. I think she is a very, lonely, young girl. I decided to see if I could befriend her instead of acting together as we had previously.

Wednesday 28th January 1953: At Bridges today, Dave and another bloke gave notice. I was beginning to get the feeling that Bridges were trying to clamp down on various aspects of the business and cut costs. They would do well in my opinion, to buy a few new machines, other than the copying lathe. I had made some changes at work myself. I had given up smoking because it was too dirty and cost too much, besides I was getting a bad cold again.

Friday 30th January 1953: I only had an efficiency of 26% at work for the week. I was not sure how that could be. I actually thought the correct figure was 126% because the extra piece-work bonus I received for the week, tallied more with the latter figure than the former. I had heard it said at Bridges that "Australians were the laziest people in the world." I decided to take no notice of this remark, which I had heard before back in Australia.

Saturday 31st January 1953: I was up early and went to the doctor who gave me some M and B tablets for my cold. Then I went on my usual Saturday jaunt into the West End. It was a very cold and blustery day. I couldn't believe it when it began to snow, sago snow. I bought some *Hansel and Gretel* records and picked up some photos, all good prints from my new camera.

In the evening I went to a YCA dance in Putney and danced with Corinne most of the night, a very elegant girl who dressed beautifully, but has a rather plain face. I felt she was someone I could talk to intelligently. I walked her home and made a date with her for next Thursday.

Sunday 1st February 1953: When I read Ma's newspaper this morning, I was surprised to read that the lowlands bordering the Thames Estuary had undergone severe flooding due to the heavy rain of the previous day, coupled with a tidal, storm surge. The weather in London, although very cold and windy, with a fall of sago snow, gave no clue to what it must have been like down at the mouth of the Thames. Ma had gone to Barbra's place, and in the afternoon Gwyn and Sylvia came over to look after me and my friends. My cold was a little better.

The mob arrived in the evening. I had bought some finger food and after we had eaten it all, we talked together in my room for a while, commenting on what a waste the double bed was. We went downstairs to watch the TV and all of us, Gwyn and Sylvia, Jean and Jim, Sheila and Brian, Ralph and me, crowded around the TV set. We watched the end of a church service, but there was much more interest in 'What's My Line.'

We thanked Gwyn and Sylvia for their hospitality and invited them to come with us to the Star and garter, but they said they were off to Barbara's to bring Mrs. Banks home. We drove off to the

Star and Garter, which they all reckoned was a great pub. We had a few beers together and then it was time for them to go back to Stevenage, So ended a very enjoyable, beaut get together. They approved of my new digs at number 22, except for the waste of a double bed.

Chapter 10
DATING CORINNE AN ELEGANT DATE

Tuesday 3rd February 1953: My sore throat was nearly better thank goodness. I went to the YCA and talked with Corinne. She was good company and was always beautifully dressed when I saw her at the YCA. She told me she was the assistant editor of *Harpers Bazaar,* a well known fashion magazine. I thought she certainly dressed appropriately for her position. I took Corinne home and we made a date to see each other again on the 5th. In 1952 none of the girls I knew, including Netta, believed that walking home by themselves, catching a bus, or the tube was risky. However, there were reports of a group of thugs called 'The Jordy Boys' who recently, had been causing a problem with bashings. That is why I always took Netta and Sylvia home and now Corinne, as well as my other dates.

Thursday 5th February 1953: I rushed my tea and went to meet Corinne. She was dressed superbly in a plaid dress with a matching Russian style hat. She looked very elegant, which made me excited to be in her company. I was dressed in my new single breasted, navy blue suit and my herringbone overcoat, so I believed I did her justice, in fact I thought we made an elegant couple. We went to the Carlton Cinema in the Haymarket and saw Danny Kaye in Hans Christian Anderson. It was a really wonderful movie, but very sad in parts. It brought back some memories of my last tour. Corinne was very quiet and I got a bit bored with her company, elegant though she was. However, she asked me to a party on Saturday week, and I gratefully accepted. What a contrast there was between her and the YCA Sylvia.

Friday 6th February 1953: I received a telegram from Len Clarkeson with his phone number. I rang him up and arranged to meet him and Netta at the Star and Garter in Putney. It was great to see Len another very good YHA friend from Melbourne, a nice bloke who bore a striking resemblance to Danny Kaye. Over a few beers at the Star and Garter, Len told us that he had been working at Rum Jungle, a uranium mining centre in the north west of the Northern Territory in Australia, where he made enough money to come over to the UK. He told us about Rum Jungle, which made me think that I might go and work there when I returned to Australia, to make some fast money. Afterwards we all came back to number 22, where they met Ralph. Ma made us a cup of tea. Ralph drove Len and Netta home and came back to sleep in the single bed that Ma had put in my room.

Sunday 8th February 1953: I read and wrote letters for most of the morning. I had to keep up with the mail because I was receiving letters nearly every day, and I tried to reply to them all. In the afternoon Ralph had gone to his dental practice. I was feeling a little lonely, so I went around to see Sylvia, but she couldn't come out with me. She told me one of her girlfriends had seen me with Corinne in Bishop's Mansions every night. I told her that wasn't true, she would only have seen me on Tuesday and Thursday night when I took Corinne home to Bishop's Mansions. The spies were out everywhere.

Monday 9th February 1953: The amount of work at Bridges was

falling off and sales were down. I wondered how much longer I would be working there. June Lucas phoned. She asked me to come over and see her on Wednesday. She wanted to know if I was broke. I hoped she didn't want me to lend her some money.

In the evening Len came over with Ralph. We went to the Star and Garter. I had been there many times before, but always in the street level bar. This time, however, Ralph led us to a bar downstairs called the Crew's Quarters. Around the walls were photographs of the various crews that had competed in the Oxford and Cambridge boat race over the years, together with many flags, oars and the like. It was a very interesting display of artifacts and memorabilia. Each year the Oxford and Cambridge boat race begins right outside the Star and Garter at Putney Bridge.

The bar surrounds too, had plenty of sporting articles that reminded me very much of the two student hotels I had visited in Heidelberg. Not only did Ralph introduce us to the Crew's Quarters, but also to a very popular game, bar billiards, played in some English hotels. We had a few beers while we waited for one of the billiard tables to become vacant and then began playing this enthralling game.

Bar billiards is based on the game of bagatelle. The game is played on a special table without side and corner pockets, but with nine holes in the playing surface. These are assigned point values from 10 to 100. There are eight balls in play, seven white and one red. The game is operated by a coin in a slot, which lasts about 15 minutes. All the shots are played from one end of the table. The game begins when a white ball is placed on the starting spot and the player uses a cue to try and get the white and remaining red balls as they come up, into the holes to score. There are various penalties too, for knocking down pegs located on the table.

The Crooked Billet pub near Brian and Sheila's house

The AA patrolman attending the Ford Consul while Ralph stands by

Canterbury Cathedral

Cover of *Porgy and Bess* program the musical I saw in the West End

The ruins of the Castle and Abbey in Ashby de la Zouch

The bar billiard table we played on at the Star and Garter hotel

I enjoyed the evening immensely, as did Len and Ralph. When Ralph took us home we both collapsed into our beds very tired. It was very good to have Ralph living at number 22 with me, but not in my bed.

Tuesday 10th February 1953: The work at Bridges was certainly slowing down. I supposed during the winter months there was not a great demand for the type of electrically driven tools that we produced for the workshop and garden, but winter was nearly at an end and the days were getting longer, so hopefully production would soon be on the rise. That night I went to the YCA meeting where I heard a Conservative MP, Mr. McTaggart, give a talk about the parliament. I didn't think he described the English parliament and its workings very well at all, however it was very interesting. I am gradually learning a little about English politics and members of parliament that I see on TV.

Wednesday 11th February 1953: There was as a trifle more work to do today at Bridges. After dinner, I went around to the nurse's flat to see June Lucas, my 'heart throb' from some time ago back in Australia. She looked a little less gaunt than when I had seen her the other day. It was a great reunion, we hugged and kissed, then settled down to swapping experiences of our tours. June had left the ship at Marseille with her friend Joan Ingles (Podge). They had toured extensively through the French Riviera, Spain, France and Austria, including Vienna. They both joined the nursing agency and were living in London at the nurse's flat with Joan, Rosemary and the others. Joan Cooper was there but did not have much to say. Of the three nurses, it was always June I dated. I was in awe of her. Thankfully June didn't ask me for a loan. Then it was back at number 22 to bed after a very exciting reunion.

Thursday 12th February 1953: After work I came home and met

Barbara's husband Chris, who had just arrived back from South Africa. He was a large man and a cynic. I didn't like him very much at all. Barbara was a different woman with her husband by her side, happy and contented. I was really happy for her.

Friday 13th February 1953: Four blokes were put off at work, certainly a 'Black Friday' for them. I couldn't see my job lasting much longer, although I had an efficiency of 122% and received a bonus of 8 shillings. After dinner Ma went out, so Ralph and I had the TV to ourselves. Joan Cooper rang up wanting a loan of my sleeping bag and parka. Ralph drove me over to the flat, where we walked into a big beer party.

Everyone was there including June. I burnt a hole in a chair and spilt a glass of beer on the carpet. It was a great night, but we missed seeing King Hussein, who had been around at the flat just before Joan rang. We smoked his gold tipped cigarettes, which he had left there on one of his many visits. I would dearly have liked to have met my 'rival.'

Chapter 11
THE CINEMA, THE BALLET, DANCING AND FOOTBALL

Sunday 15th February 1953: Ralph was in Stevenage and in the afternoon I went over to Netta's and had tea with her friend Pam, a South African. We three then went into the West End and saw *Plymouth Adventure*, another movie released the previous year starring Spencer Tracy, Gene Tierney and Van Johnson. The movie was about the pilgrims on the *Mayflower*, quite interesting, but I am not very fond of historical movies. It was nice to be with the girls. The outing finished with coffee at their flat, after which I went back home to bed.

Monday 16th February 1953: I went to the cinema in Putney to see *Limelight* starring Charlie Chaplin and Claire Bloom, both magnificent in their roles. Charlie Chaplin produced and directed this great movie. He was a remarkable man and Claire Bloom was truly beautiful. I decided not to go to the YCA meeting tomorrow night as this week's program looked a little boring.

Wednesday 18th February 1953: I had developed a horrible pimple on my nose. I tried to make it a little more presentable, but I only made it worse and it hurt like hell. I met Ralph at King's Cross and we went to Covent Garden to see the ballet. We sat in the grand tier, which cost 22/6, but I thought my usual seats, four rows back in the stalls were better to view the ballet performance and cheaper. Moira Shearer was the principal ballerina, but I didn't know that when she was on stage. We had arranged to meet Netta and Pam in the foyer after the show. Ralph drove us all back to Netta's and we didn't leave there until 2 a.m., after a very enjoyable night, except for my nose, which was very sore. I didn't know the names of the ballet dancers we saw, except Moira Shearer.

I picked up a copy of a free booklet called *What's On In London,* published each week. It listed all the shows that were on in the West End, as well as all the other events for the week. It also listed 'old' movies that could be seen at local cinemas around London. Each week these movies shifted around to different suburban cinemas. From time to time, new old movies were added and some removed. There was often an old movie, (most released no more than 10 years ago) that I wished to see and enjoy again, especially if it was being shown in Putney or Hammersmith, or other nearby cinema.

Thursday 19th February 1953: After work and dinner I went to the cinema in Putney and saw *The Fleet's In* starring Dorothy Lamour and Betty Hutton, a movie I had seen advertised in *What's On In London.* The movie was released in 1942. I had seen it before during the war years, when I skipped class at the Melbourne Working Man's College. Each week I searched *What's On In London,* to see what other great films of earlier years, were being resurrected.

Friday 20th February 1953: I went to Bridges Social Club dance. Even though I was by myself it was an enjoyable night, but certainly not up to the Harrods standard of a social occasion, a dinner suit was not required. I had quite a few beers and danced with an attractive girl called Marj, who I was going to ask to take home, but discovered she was married.

Saturday 21st February 1953: I went to Putney in the morning and bought a light blue jumper for 17 shillings. I had been looking for just such a jumper for quite a while, one I saw worn by an actor in a movie, but could never see the exact style and colour I wanted. After lunch I met Ralph at King's Cross and we went to a game of soccer between Tottenham Hotspurs (the Spurs) and Preston. The entry price was 7 shillings. The game ended in a 'one all draw.' I enjoyed the game but, the trouble with English soccer is that there are long periods where nothing much happens. When it does, such as a goal being scored, or some player getting 'injured', the reaction from the players and the crowd is a sporting orgasm. Sadly however, there aren't too many multiple orgasms in the game of soccer.

A draw in Australian Rules football only occurs occasionally, but with soccer it is quite common. I was also quite amazed to see, when an English soccer player went down with what appeared to me to be a trifling injury, which in Australian Rules football would be virtually ignored, the soccer player puts on such an unmanly performance, one would think he had been mortally wounded.

Back home to Ma for dinner. Afterwards Ralph and I met Sheila and Jean and took them to the ballet at Covent Garden. It was *The Sleeping Beauty*, also danced under the name of *The Sleeping Princess*. The principal dancers were Brian Shaw, Phillip Chatfield and Violetta Elvin. They all gave superb performances. As arranged, we returned to Sheila's place in Ralph's Consul. Brian and Jim returned from London in the Morris much later in the night. Brian and Jim don't like the ballet so they went to the movies, a nightclub, or other entertainment in the West End. Both groups making their way back separately to Stevenage after the shows. Ralph and I slept in the double bed again, but this time thankfully, he didn't mistake me for Gladys. We had a good night's sleep after a busy day.

Sunday 22nd February 1953: After breakfast Ralph and I helped Brian clean out Ralph's new, large hot house boilers, which he had built for his expanding hot house business, while I was away on my second tour. It was a hot, dirty and wet job. Brian showed me around the greenhouses again, where I was amazed to see such a large collection of vegetables, tomatoes, lettuce, cucumber, and many others, all growing in the hot, humid, environment. When we had finished on the boilers, we had a few beers and a game of darts at the Crooked Billet. I was getting better at darts the more I played, which was very encouraging. Then it was back to Sheila's for a tasty dinner and a lazy afternoon. In the evening we all went to Percy's Brewhouse in Bedford. We had a randy time there and some of the jokes that were told were really filthy, but it was good fun if you have a broad mind, which I have.

Monday 23rd February 1953: Up before 7 a.m. and away with Ralph in the Consul to London, where I clocked on at Bridges at 10 a.m. It was a lousy day at work because I was very tired. I came home, wrote to my parents and watched TV, which was so relaxing, interesting and novel, even though the size of the screen is only twelve inches wide and black and white.

Tuesday 24th February 1953: Dinner over, I went around to wish Netta, Nellie and Noel goodbye and bon voyage. They were all leaving for the Continent in the morning, and would not be back until the third week in May. It was a lovely farewell evening. I will really miss Netta, not being able to phone or call round to visit her, although Pam would still be there. Netta asked me to pick up her skis and case and hold them for her. She said she would write to me, to tell me when and where they were. This was the second time I missed going to the YCA.

Thursday 26th February 1953: I went to the cinema in Putney and saw *The Third Man,* which was terrific in every way. When I was in Vienna on my first tour, I was very aware that it was the location for the movie, released in 1949. While I was there I dined at the *Althofkeller,* a restaurant where the cast and technicians from the movie frequently dined, and where there was a zither player, who played the theme tune of *The Third Man.* I saw the huge Ferris wheel in Prater, the amusement park that was featured in the movie. Some of the movie was shot in Vienna's underground sewers.

It was very exciting for me to see this movie because apart from my association with its location, it is a brilliant movie with an enthralling story and wonderful actors, Orson Welles, Joseph Cotton, Trevor Howard and Alida Valli. I imagined I was back in Vienna again as it was all so realistic. When I came home I wrote to May about what I had been doing since I last wrote to her.

Saturday 28th February 1953: A beautiful day in more ways than one. Tomorrow would be the first day of spring. I was really looking forward to the longer days and brighter weather. I shopped in Putney in the morning and after lunch I walked along the Thames upstream from Putney Bridge, finishing up at the Fulham football ground, a pleasant walk in the weak sun. In the evening I decided it was time I blessed the Hammersmith Palais with my presence again, as I had not been there for a few weeks.

I resisted the temptation to dress down, but dressed in my best suit as usual. I was glad I did so, because I met a very lovely girl, a blonde shorter than me, with blue eyes and nail paint. Her name was Pamela and she didn't chew gum. We danced together to

Victor Sylvester's music. She was just gorgeous. I was smitten. I made a date to see her next Wednesday, but she wouldn't let me take her home.

Sunday 1st March 1953: I woke late on this first day of spring and rang Pam, Netta's African friend to see if she would like to go a walk with me in the afternoon. "Love Too," she said. We walked along the Chelsea Embankment and across the Albert Bridge, a rusty, combination cantilever and suspension bridge that led us to Battersea Park. The Chelsea Embankment extends from the Chelsea Bridge to the Albert Bridge on the north bank of the Thames. The Thames looked very dirty, but I believe that in the last 40 years it has been cleaned up, so much so, that fish can now be caught in this vicinity. Looking across the river, the tall chimneys and buildings of the Battersea Power Station could be seen, a slight wisp of smoke or steam coming from the chimneys. We retraced our steps back to the Embankment where we had a meal together, then went to a movie in Balham.

After the movie, which was quite good, we returned to Pam's place and talked about everything until 8.30 p.m. Pam came from Cape Town and was not really a backpacker, but came to the UK to gain work experience in accounting. She is a very attractive, young lady, about my age and good company, but I was looking forward to Wednesday when I meet the other Pam.

Chapter 12
DATING A TONI TWIN AND A PUZZLING NOISE

Tuesday 3rd March 1953: I was woken when it was still dark by a loud unearthly whining. I wondered what the hell it was. I went to the YCA meeting where my boss, Mr. Bridges was to give a talk, but he didn't turn up. He left a message apologising and saying that he was trying to land a contract. I hoped for mine and the company's sake that he was successful. Instead we played table tennis, but I didn't play for long, because it became very dusty, making me feel sick. This saved me making up my mind whether I should ask to take Sylvia or Corinne home.

Wednesday 4th March 1953: Once again, at about the same time as last night, I was woken by the same whining, eerie sound, as I heard the previous night. It seemed to come from overhead, but if it was a plane, I had never heard one like that before. After dinner I cleaned up and went on the fast, Piccadilly Line tube train from Earl's Court to Acton where I met Pamela. That was a good start, because I had been stood up so many times. We went to the Q Theatre where we saw *The Innocents*, starring Ann Crawford, but we didn't think it was very good. Afterwards we went to a pub for a drink. We both drank beer. Pamela told me she was one of the 'Toni Twins.' I had seen advertisements for the Toni Twins many times on Ma's TV and in the press. I had seen these advertisements many times in Australia too, in magazines, on billboards and at the movies.

Pamela explained to me what that was all about. Pamela had long, blonde hair, quite unlike a Toni permanent wave as seen in the advertisements. Toni was a company that sold 'do it yourself hair permanent wave kits,' which cost 8/3. To demonstrate how good their product was, the company recruited beautiful twin girls, giving one an expensive permanent wave by a hairdresser. The other twin was given an identical style, using the 'do it yourself' Toni method. The twins were then shown side by side with the catch phrase, 'Which twin has the Toni?'

Of course, one could not tell the difference between the two hair styles. The advertisement never disclosed the answer. I asked Pamela if she was the one with or without the Toni. She said that sometimes she was, or her twin sister. After I returned to Australia, I again saw the advertisements many times, and even though I looked closely, I never recognised Pamela in any of them, but they certainly revived some enigmatic memories.

Thursday 5th March 1953: I asked some of the blokes at work if they had heard the same sounds as I had heard the last two nights. One said it was most likely one of the new *Comet* jets coming in to land or taking off from one of London's airports. When I was travelling by double-decker bus from Stevenage to London, I could look over the fence of the de Havilland Aircraft Company's airfield and factory at Hatfield, where I was able to get a brief glimpse of these beautifully, streamlined, silver aircraft, gleaming in the sun. The puzzle was solved.

The story of the *Comet* is an epic in the history of the development of a pure jet, long haul, passenger aircraft. It was developed at Hatfield by de Havilland and flew for the first time in

1949. From that time on it was under continuous development, including trial flights to Rome, Copenhagen, and Cairo. It was considered to be so airworthy that Queen Elizabeth II, the Queen Mother and Princess Margaret took a flight around Europe in May 1952,

Later in 1952, it flew to celebrations in Southern Rhodesia. Everything about the *Comet* that I had seen over the fence at Hatfield and in photographs was wonderful. It was a sleek, aircraft, much more beautiful and feminine than today's 747 jumbos. One aspect of the design that made them look so sleek and feminine, was that the four jet engines, were enclosed within the wings and not mounted below the wings on pods, like the very masculine 747s and 737s. The *Comet* was accident free, except for some minor early accidents without loss of life, after which the cause was quickly found and rectified.

De Havilland was an aircraft brand name that I knew about from the time I was a young boy. A large, beautiful plane flew over our house on many occasions. My father said it was a de Havilland *Rapide* flying into Essendon Airport, bringing mail and passengers from Tasmania. It was a classic aircraft, a large bodied, twin-engine biplane, with a fixed undercarriage housed in spats below the engines.

From the TV, I learned that Stalin, the Premier of the USSR, died today at the age of 73. His death marked the beginning of the 'cold war' in world politics, especially in the relationship between Russia and America. I wondered what Stalin's death would mean for the big powers and whether it would lead to a more peaceful world.

Friday 6th March 1953: My efficiency for this week was given as only 30%. I was sure this was incorrect, so I went and saw my foreman. We had a frank discussion about the company, me, the machines, the method of deducing the week's efficiency, and being short paid, as I had been on a couple of occasions and other problems. We spoke for over an hour. He said the 30% should have been 130% and he would have it corrected in my next pay. He told me Bridges had signed a contract, which would secure the future of the company. That was really good news. After our discussion I think we understood each other a lot better.

Ralph came home and told me and Ma Banks that he would be leaving in the morning. He had managed to get a room on the other side of the city. That was great news: Now I could have my room to myself. Not that Ralph had been any problem, but it was not ideal sharing a room with another person who had different daily schedules.

Saturday 7th March 1953: I met Pamela in the afternoon and we went and watched the football at Chelsea. It was a farce of a game, a nil-all-draw. Ma Banks, who seemed to like Pamela put on dinner for us both, which was very generous of her. Then we went off to the ballet at Covent Garden. I was a little sorry because Pamela wasn't really dressed for the ballet. When we walked down the aisle to our seats, I noticed that her clothes looked a little grubby. It was my fault, because I didn't decide to take her to the ballet until late in the afternoon.

The ballets were *Les Patineurs (The Skaters)* and *The Shadow*, both of which I enjoyed, but I was not sure what Pamela thought of the ballet because she didn't say much, but I thought she enjoyed it. Afterwards, she said that it was the first time she had been to the ballet and to Covent Garden. I wasn't really sure what my feelings were for Pamela, except that they were certainly not the same as when I first met her, although I was happy to be in her company.

She was beautiful with her long, blonde hair, not styled in a tight perm as in the Toni advertisements.

Sunday 8th March 1953: I spent the afternoon reading, then after dinner I went out to Pamela's house in Acton, but I was not invited inside. I took her to the cinema. Then we went to a cafe for a drink, where I asked her a few questions about herself. She had said she was divorced, but said she was not actually divorced yet, her divorce was not due until August. Pamela said she liked me a lot and that I was the nicest chap she had ever met, but I couldn't be invited into her house; because her mother wouldn't permit it. Her mother probably wanted to ensure that nothing jeopardised her daughter's upcoming divorce. I told Pamela I still wanted to see her, so we made a date for next Wednesday. I wasn't sure if I should have broken it off there and then. I liked her very much, but I was not sure how genuine she was and the relationship was getting a little too complicated.

Monday 9th March 1953: Netta sent me a letter from Austria, where she was skiing. Ralph and I had decided to meet each Monday night at the Star and Garter Crew's Quarters to have a few drinks and play bar billiards. I told Ralph all about Pamela and he said he envied me. He said I was a very lucky bloke to be going out with a girl like her, but to be *very careful*. I said I would. We parted after having a few beers and a couple of games of bar billiards.

Tuesday 10th March 1953: I got a long letter from my mother. At last they have got the record I cut at HMV, which of course would have been five weeks ago! My mother said the family all crowded around while the record was playing. She said it was wonderful to hear my voice and was glad that I spoke about Auntie Ruby and all the relations in Glasgow. When I returned to Australia in listened to the record I had made a couple of times, and was very pleased how it sounded. It was money very well spent.

Joan Cooper rang up and by what she said and the tone of her voice, I think she wanted me to make a date with her. I was too involved with Pamela to think about Joan, Corinne or Sylvia. I will ring her later perhaps. I finally got to YCA and had a short time there, before I came back to number 22 and wrote to my mother before I went to bed.

Wednesday 11th March 1953: Even though I have another lousy cold, I met Pamela and we went again to the Q Theatre in Acton Vale where we saw the movie *Worms Eye View,* a comedy about billeted RAF recruits, starring big busted Diana Dors. Pamela insisted on paying for the tickets. I thought she was marvellous. I had never met a girl who liked my company as much as she did. Except of course Netta. It was a beaut feeling. She told me that her husband was in jail. What next, I thought. I didn't think she was in love with me, and as attractive as she was, I certainly wasn't in love with her. She intrigued me and I had to wonder what my future was with her.

Chapter 13
ABLUTIONS AND THE END OF THE TONI TWIN

Friday 13th March 1953: Black Friday again. I went to Putney straight after work and bought a small radio, as there were many good programs on BBC radio that I was sure I would enjoy. I came home to number 22, and after dinner I prepared for my weekly bath. Ma didn't allow me to fill the bath to the usual level, because she said that the gas bill was too high. She said the cost of living had risen, and that when I left, she would have two people in my room. I think she liked the extra board money she received, when Ralph was staying at number 22.

The weekly bath night was the norm for most working class people living in English houses in those times. Very few had showers, only baths, hot water being provided by a gas heater in the bathroom. Many people like me washed their bodies with a sponge during the week. This, coupled with a liberal application of deodorant insured that one's body odour was acceptable. I was careful to make sure my hands and nails were clean and well manicured, which is not always easy for a fitter and turner. I was always aware of the lovely perfumes worn by the girls I dated, which helped to disguise their body odour.

I also had weekly baths in my parents' house in Rosanna. We didn't have a hot water service, our bath water was heated by a wood chip heater. Although there was a shower above the bath, it was only connected to the cold water supply. The only time I used the shower was prior to going skiing for two weeks with the Rover Scouts. I had a cold shower each day, under the misguided idea that it would toughen my body to endure the cold when I was skiing, but I don't think it did.

For anyone who wanted more than the weekly bath, there were municipal baths, not for swimming, but for personal ablutions. A small fee was charged for the use of the hot shower and bath. Most were also equipped with massage and Turkish baths. Before I left to go skiing to Mt Buller, after coming from work, I used one in Melbourne's Spencer Street railway station, but it didn't have massage or Turkish bath facilities. A towel and a locker were provided.

I was never sure how Ralph kept himself clean for his dental surgery; quite possibly, he frequented a municipal bath. Brian and Sheila's house in Stevenage had a hot water service and a bathroom with a shower. When I stayed there, it was Heaven to stand under the hot shower and wash away all the deodorant and English dirt. It was not until I returned to Australia and began working for the State Electricity Commission (SEC) that I was able to have a hot shower each day, in the single men's accommodation block of the camp where I was living.

Saturday 14th March 1953: Pamela rang and said she wasn't very well, so I decided to go to the football by myself at the Fulham footy ground. This game between Fulham and Nottingham was a particularly, mind numbing spectacle. Watching the ball moving continually from one end of the pitch to the other, with the occasional player being brought to ground, accompanied with the usual writhing around, pretending to be badly hurt. I left early to pick up Pamela and didn't even bother to look in the paper the next day to see what the final score was.

I met Pamela and took her round to have tea with Ma, who enjoyed her company and was very interested to learn that she was one of the Toni Twins, asking her many questions about her work. As Pamela wasn't feeling well, we just went to the movies at Putney and saw *Sousa Marching Along*, a movie about the famous American brass band leader, John Sousa. It was an interesting movie, but I am not really an admirer of brass band music. I took Pamela home, leaving her with a goodnight kiss.

Sunday 15th March 1953: A lovely sunny day. In the afternoon I took Pamela, who was feeling much better to the London Zoo, located a short distance north of London in a section of Regents Park. I hadn't been to a zoo for many years, except for the one in Milan. The London Zoo, opened in 1847. It has a large variety of animals, including a few kangaroos. I felt sorry for them, especially during these winter months. In the Zoo's early years it had a large elephant named 'Jumbo.' The word jumbo subsequently became a synonym for an elephant.

We left the zoo because it had become very cold. We went into the West End and had a meal in a cafe. Then we saw the movie *The Tales of Hoffman* at the La Scala. I had seen the movie before, but certainly didn't mind seeing it again. Many in the audience were wearing little black caps perched on the back of their heads, indicating they were Jews. Except that the composer Offenbach was a Jew, I couldn't quite see what drew so many Jews to see this movie. Afterwards we retired to a pub and drank 'Stingos' a double strength beer and brown ales.

While we were drinking our beers, Pamela whispered to me, "I want to go to bed with you." I was startled by her revelation, replying with a tentative whisper, "Yes that would be that be nice," and left it at that. I was of course flattered, while quickly thinking to myself that it wasn't possible, unless I was to take her away somewhere for the weekend or a night to a hotel. It certainly wasn't going to happen in my room at number 22 that were for sure. We left the pub a little merry and had a pleasant ride home in the tube, falling into each other's arms behind a not very elegant, back fence.

As I lay in bed that night I gave Pamela's whispered wish some thought. It would be very exciting to go to bed with Pamela, but I wondered if it would be 'worth the trouble' as it were. Besides, I was not really convinced of her motives, or feelings for me, so I resolved to sleep on it, but not with Pamela, not at the moment anyway.

Tuesday 17th March 1953: I received a message to contact the Orient Line. I did so and booked my dinner table seat on the *Orion*. This I thought was quite peculiar; because I wasn't going to be joining the ship for another three months. Ma Banks had caught my cold and went off to bed. I watched the TV for a while, where I saw that Tito, the communist president of Yugoslavia, had just arrived in London.

I went to the YCA meeting, where Mr. Bridges gave a very interesting talk about industry in the UK. I thought he was a little nervous and although we had said hullo to each other at work, I didn't think he recognised me at the meeting. Most probably because a YCA meeting I was sure, would be the last place he would expect to see one of his employees.

Wednesday 18th March 1953: After work and dinner, I met Pamela at the Clarendon Hammersmith hotel for a drink together with some of her girlfriends. They were quite pleasant and we talked for a while. They wanted to know all about Australia and what I had been doing since I left there. I gave them a vague idea of my exploits and left it at that, although they were very interested.

Leaving there, Pamela and I went to the Hammersmith Palais close by. We danced a lot, but I never really enjoyed it. We didn't talk too much while we danced. I was very relieved, when we decided to leave and get out in the fresh air. I took Pamela home and on the way back to her place, we talked a lot. I told her about my imagined plans for the future. We parted with a kiss and plans for our next date next Sunday. On the way back to Number 22, I got the feeling she was laughing at me. Meeting with her girlfriends, was just to show me off.

Thursday 19th March 1953: After work when I got home, I found that Mrs. Banks was quite ill. I got my own dinner, while she went off to bed. I watched TV and saw Shakespeare's *As You Like It*. I did like it, especially as I remembered doing this play in school. On the TV I saw an amazing atom blast test in the USA, which disintegrated a mock house. I also saw Tito at a big air display.

Friday 20th March 1953: I got my own breakfast in the morning and when I came home from work Sylvia was with her mother. I was glad to see that Ma Banks was much better. Sylvia told me that her mother wanted Saturdays to herself. She would like me to look after myself on Saturdays in future. After Sylvia left I gave it a bit of thought. Barbara rang and followed up on her mother's wishes. She asked me if I could organize myself, so as make sure her mum's Saturdays were free. I said I would, no problem.

Saturday 21st March 1953: I was going to meet Pamela in the afternoon, but Ralph came, so we picked up Pamela and went to Twickenham, where we saw England beat the Scots at rugby. It was a lousy game, but infinitely better to watch than soccer or football as they call it. For a change of scene and entertainment, we went into the West End. We decided to go to the ballet at Covent Garden. We saw *Swan Lake*, which was great, but I couldn't concentrate fully on the ballet because I didn't know if Pamela was enjoying it very much. As before, she never said much. After we took Pamela home, I told Ralph about her saying she wanted to go to bed with me. He said, "Half your luck mate, but be careful." "I don't think it is going to happen, but thanks for the advice." I replied.

Sunday 22nd March 1953: After dinner I met Pamela, who said she would like to go skating. I was pleased that she had asked me to take her somewhere where she, wanted to go. We went to the skating rink at Richmond. I fell and hurt my bum, but Pamela was a good skater and enjoyed herself immensely. Afterwards we had a meal at a café where, after seemingly having such a good time on the ice, Pamela unburdened herself regarding our relationship.

She began saying, "You are conceited and have an inferiority complex." Where had I heard that before, I thought. She went on to say, "I don't like football or the ballet." There was more. "I wear a cap and have been aborted." She finished with a final revelation. "All I want is to get drunk in a man's flat and go to bed with him. That's my idea of a pleasant evening!" I just sat there flabbergasted. I couldn't believe it. I looked at her and said. "It's about time I took you home." She agreed saying. "Yes I think you better; because we have nothing in common." I took her home and we parted with a kiss.

On the way back to number 22 in the bus my mind was full of the things Pamela had just told me. As soon as I was in my room, I wrote up my diary, entering all the failings she had ascribed to me, and the things she didn't like. I pondered over each item, as I wrote them down. I couldn't understand how conceitedness and an inferiority complex were compatible.

This was the second time I had been told I had an inferiority complex by a girlfriend, first Netta and now Pamela. I was not surprised she didn't like football, although I was sure she would have liked Australian Rules. I wasn't very surprised that she had been aborted, especially when she said. "Getting drunk in a man's flat and ending up in bed," was her idea of a pleasant evening. I had to admit, that our last date was the first time that she had said what she wanted to do. That is of course, other than go to bed with me. On all of our other dates, I had made the decision where we would go. Most it seemed were not to her liking. It all added up.

There was one item Pamela told me about herself that puzzled me. "I wear a cap." I thought at the time she must have meant that she wore a blonde wig, and as she was one of the *Toni Twins* that was what it was. I was sure however that she was not wearing a wig when I was dating her. It was not until some 50 years later when I was married and was typing this statement into the word processor that I suddenly realised that the 'cap' she was referring to was a contraceptive. She could have added to her list of items about my failings that I was extremely naïve, and indeed I was. In some matters, anyhow.

I thought there was no doubt that travel had broadened my mind in visiting foreign countries with their vastly different languages, landscapes and cultures, many very different from those of my home country. Also broadened, was my knowledge of the difference in personalities of the eligible and not so eligible, young, English women I had dated.

Monday 23rd March 1953: After work Ralph came around and we went to the Star and Garter. I told him all about the happenings over the last couple of days at number 22 and with Pamela. He said I have to find a new place to board. As regards Pamela, Ralph reckoned I got out of it lightly. I agreed. We had a good night playing bar billiards before going back to number 22. I really didn't know what to do about looking for new board, except to 'sleep on it' and that's exactly what I did.

I had a letter from Netta telling me all about her travels. Her letter really cheered me up. Netta asked me to pick up her skis and case at Victoria railway station in the next few days.

Chapter 14
A ROYAL FUNERAL AND TO THE BALLET

Tuesday 24th March 1953: The Dowager Queen Mary died on this day aged 86. She knew that she was approaching death and left specific instructions. 'If she died before the coronation, court mourning was not to interfere with the date or celebrations of that great day.' Queen Mary married the Duke of York in 1892. In 1911 they were crowned King George V and Queen Mary. King George V died in 1936. I remembered them both, from seeing many photos of them in my childhood.

Saturday 28th March 1953: I rose early and picked up Netta's case and skis at Victoria Street Station. Then I went to Putney Bridge and watched the start of the Oxford and Cambridge boat race from the north bank of the Thames. I followed the race for a kilometre, but the boats moved too fast for me, so I decided to run home and watch the remainder on TV. Cambridge won easily. In the evening I went to the Star and Garter to a dance where I had a great time amongst the people who had been at the race.

The Oxford and Cambridge Boat Race was first held in 1829, starting from Henley. The start was moved to Putney Bridge in 1856. The race is an annual event raced over a distance of 6.4 km, from Putney Bridge to Mortlake, with each boat crew having eight rowers and a coxswain. Cambridge has won the race more times than Oxford. Putney Bridge, which I have crossed over so many times was originally a wooden bridge erected in 1729. It was the third London bridge to span the Thames. A classic, iron arch bridge replaced the wooden span in 1886. It is of the same design as our Princes Bridge that spans the Yarra in Melbourne.

Sunday 29th March 1953: There was so much happening in London this year, and now the sad death of the Dowager Queen. I went along to Whitehall where I saw Queen Mary's funeral procession. Her coffin was carried on the Horse Guards gun carriage. Luckily I managed to get directly in front of the gate of Whitehall, which was great because I particularly wanted to see her son, the Duke of Windsor (who abdicated in 1936 to marry Mrs. Simpson). I was standing beside all the TV and movie cameras, so I had a good view, but just missed seeing him when I took a couple of photos. It was really a significant moment to be amongst the mourning people of London most like me, Londoners.

I bought a couple of tickets for the ballet and as Netta was away I decided to ring Marjorie, a beautiful brunette to see if she would like to come to the ballet with me, on Tuesday, instead of going to the YCA. She said she would love to. We had talked together at club nights about the ballet and other things, so I thought that she would be an ideal choice. She was the young lady who made a point of asking me to come back next week at the close of my first YCA meeting.

Monday 30th March 1953: I had a terrific argument with the boss, the old bastard (not Mr. Bridges) about the lousy machines and the terrible working conditions. After the events at work that day, I thought seriously, not only of looking for another job, but also, of leaving number 22 and Ma Banks. After dinner Ralph came over and we rang the nurses to see if any of them wanted to go pub crawling. The only two at home were Rosemary Roberts and Joan Cooper. They said they would love to. Ralph picked them up and we went to a few pubs close by including The Boathouse, a beaut pub by the Thames.

We had a hilarious time and on the way home, Ralph got lost in the back streets. As he edged his way along, another car hit us from the side, not very hard and no one was hurt. While Ralph was sorting things out with the other driver, the two girls in the back seat were giggling like mad and rattling beer bottles on the car floor. I had to go and tell them sternly to "Shut Up!" Ralph and the other driver agreed that it was just an unavoidable accident. We went back to the nurse's flat, where we had a few more drinks before we went home. It was altogether a scream of a night.

Tuesday 31st March 1953: I met Marjorie and off we went to Covent Garden in the bus. We saw *Les Sylphides, Checkmate* and *Mademoiselle Angot.* Alicia Markova danced *Les Sylphides* beautifully, she just floated. After the performance we went to the stage door, where we managed to get Alicia Markova's autograph, as well as a couple of others. We saw Markova driven away in her chauffeur driven Rolls Royce, and then we made our way back home.

I was particularly thrilled by the ballet *Checkmate,* even though I didn't know the game of chess on which the ballet is based. The stage was set out as a chess board and all the dancers represented chess pieces, pawns, knights, kings and queens. *Mademoiselle Angot (Mam'zelle Angot)* was a delightful ballet and of course *Les Sylphides* was out of this world. Marjorie was lovely company. I would have liked to ask her out again, but she was dating another bloke in the YCA and there was no way I would try to butt in on that. Was that my inferiority complex taking control, I wondered?

Chapter 15
EASTER IN STEVENAGE

Thursday 2nd April 1953: I had my weekly bath one day early because I had been invited to spend Easter with Sheila and Brian at Stevenage. After dinner Ralph picked me up and off we went in the pouring rain along the Great North Road to their house, where we spent the evening talking and having a few beers.

Friday 3rd April 1953: Good Friday. After breakfast on a nice sunny morning, I helped Brian work on the boilers. Lunch over, we had a restful afternoon. In the evening we went to a pub in Hitchin. Then it was off to Jim and Jean's place to look at the TV they had just bought. On the TV, much to Jim and Brian's displeasure, the first program was about the ballet, with Markova in *Les Sylphides*. Jean and Sheila, myself and Ralph were quite happy, but we had to put up with Jim and Brian's critical comments all through the show. It was fun though, with exactly their same reaction as when they visited me and had a look at Mrs. Banks TV, when a church service was the first program they saw.

Saturday 4th April 1953: I worked on the boilers with Brian. It was dirty but enjoyable work. I felt that in a small way, I was repaying them for the wonderful hospitality they had extended to me during my time in England. In the evening we all went to the Cherry Tree pub at Welwyn Garden City, where we had a very enjoyable time. There were 16 in our party, all friends of Brian and Sheila. Thankfully, on the way home the road wasn't fog bound like the last time.

Sunday 5th April 1953: I worked on the boilers again during the day. In the evening we went to a pub called The Bull in Whitwell, a very picturesque, small village, like so many other small English villages and their local pubs. We drank and played darts, and once again it was a great night with all my friends. We danced, drank and made merry.

Monday 6th April 1953: On the boilers again, the work consisting of such jobs as cleaning the grate, firebox, fire tubes, smoke box and polishing the brass work. Much the same type of maintenance required on a locomotive boiler, with which I was very familiar. After a shower and lunch I caught the train back to London, after an Easter holiday that I thoroughly enjoyed with my English friends.

Chapter 16
I LOOK FOR NEW BOARD

Wednesday 8th April 1953: For quite a while, I had been thinking of trying to find a new boarding house with full board. I had worked over in my mind what sort of alternative board I wanted. As well as being better than my conditions at number 22, which really would be hard to beat, it had to be one that I would be able to have anyone I wished visit me in my room, especially of course a member of the female sex. I mentioned my intention to Ralph. "Good idea mate," he said.

Not long ago when I talked on the phone to Joan Cooper, I told her I was looking for new board as I wanted some privacy. As we talked I couldn't help myself saying, "Wouldn't it be beaut, if we could spend the night together?" Without a moment's hesitation she said, "If you find a place, we can!" Now if that wasn't an incentive, I don't know what was?

I decided to give myself a fortnight or three weeks to see if I could find what I wanted. I had a look at a few places advertised in shop windows in the general area. After work, I continued searching, but sadly with no success. I continued searching for a couple of weeks, but still could not find any that were suitable in providing full board, a nice private room and good facilities.

It was wonderful to have my own radio. I listened to many

diverse programs on both the first (or light) program and the third program, commonly referred to as the 'arts program.' On the third program I heard Orson Welles narrating *A Song of Myself*, a long, long poem, by American poet Walt Whitman with the theme 'In Celebration of Himself,' which was truly enthralling, especially being read by Orson Welles in his deep melodious voice.

Saturday 11th April 1953: I went shopping in the morning and realised that it must be spring, because the flowers were beginning to bloom. After dinner I went to a UYCA (United YCA) dance and spent a lot of money on beer, raffle tickets and the like. I was sorry I didn't go to the Palais instead. Sylvia looked lovely and was very friendly.

The night finished at a horrible party at Frank's place, another UYCA member. The music was very loud and not at all to my liking, so I went home by myself with a stomach full of beer.

Sunday 12th April 1953: It was raining heavily. I looked up *What's On In London* and saw there was a good movie *Never Let Me Go* showing in the cinema in Putney, so off I went. The film starred Clark Gable and Gene Tierney. It was a great movie about a newspaper correspondent in communist Russia. After the movie we were treated to a short documentary demonstrating *3D Metroscopics*. It was very intriguing looking at the screen in 3D with the special glasses that were provided. I wondered if that was how we would see movies in the future. Back home at number 22. I saw *L'Aiglon (Young Eagle)* on the TV, a story about Bonaparte's son in Vienna and Schonbrunn, which of course I found extremely interesting.

Tuesday 14th April 1953: On the way home from work I inspected a few more boarding rooms, but without success. In the end I decided I had no option, but to stay with Mrs. Banks who had

A De Havilland *Comet*

The game in progress at the Twickenham Football Ground

A Toni Twins advertisement. Pamela is not one of these girls

The Oxford and Cambridge boat race just after the start

Brian Day's new boiler house for the greenhouses

The Dowager Queen Mary's coffin emerging from Whitehall

Beautiful Marjorie from YCA, I took to the ballet

really been good to me and kept me out of trouble. I realised in fact, how fortunate I was, to have found Mrs. Banks and her house, so quickly. Not forgetting too that I was now a member of the greater Banks family, which was an important factor that I considered in my deliberations.

After dinner I went to the YCA meeting, where there was not much on except talking amongst ourselves and playing table tennis. Apart from finding Ma Banks, I was also very fortunate to have seen the advertisement for the YCA. By joining the Association, I was able to really immerse myself in leading the life of a young Londoner. Not only was I having a full and interesting social life but, the YCA had enabled me to learn a lot about politics in Great Britain, both local and national.

When I returned from my second tour, I had no intention of living in London with only Australian friends in an Australian ghetto like 'Kangaroo Valley.' The district of Earl's Court, was given this nickname; because many itinerant and expatriate Australians lived in that area. I was sure that in the last six months I had achieved an ideal balance for my social and working life as 'An Aussie Backpacking Londoner.'

Wednesday 15th April 1953: Watching TV after YCA, I saw our Test cricketers. They were over here for the test series to begin in June. It was good to see our boys on the screen, Hassett the captain, Morris, Miller, Lindwall, Harvey, Davidson and a couple of others. I tried to make a date with June Lucas a couple of times since she had arrived in London, but apart from seeing her once at the nurse's flat, I hadn't had any luck. Talking to Joan Cooper on the phone, I discovered that June came to England on the same ship as the Australian cricket team. June was dating Ken Miller the Australian batsman, she met on the ship. Inferiority complex or not,

I was not going to attempt to win June away from a very successful test cricketer. However I did not feel inferior to him at all. He was a very good cricketer, as I was a skier.

Thursday 16th April 1953: Len Clarkeson invited me out to his flat in Hampstead, saying he had a big surprise for me. I asked if I could bring Ralph and of course he said yes. I had been including Ralph in all the contacts I had with my YHA friends here, just as he had done for me with his friends in Stevenage. It certainly was a surprise when the door opened to see Betty Nutting, Gwen Greensill (Leon Langley's heart throb), Elizabeth Loughlan and Lin Coughlin, all members of YHA in Melbourne. It was so thrilling to see them again. I introduced Ralph to them all. Then we all got down to swapping our experiences. Elizabeth Loughnan told us she and Gwen Greensill left Melbourne in December 1952, on the last voyage of the SS *Maloja*, which kept breaking down.

They left the *Maloja* at Marseilles and hitchhiked up through France to Lyon and to Geneva in Switzerland. From there they went to Bad Gastein in Austria and spent a marvellous week skiing there. Then they went through Italy to Venice, Pompeii, Naples and Capri. Along the way they met up with Lin Coughlin, another YHA member from Melbourne. After leaving Venice, they spent some time in Rome. From then on, they decided to only accept a ride in a vehicle with a single driver, because of an unpleasant episode they had with a couple of 'Italian Romeos.' Elizabeth and Gwen returned to London for Easter, via Spain, which they found was very expensive. They both found jobs at Marks and Spencers in London.

Everyone who was there at Len's place said that they had booked a seat for the Coronation and were looking forward to the once in a lifetime event, with great excitement. At the end of the wonderful reunion, I made a date with Betty Nutting to take her to the Hammersmith Palais next month to dance to Victor Sylvester's dance band, which she said, was her favourite band. She gave me her phone number. I said I would ring her when I made sure of the night the band was playing.

Before I dropped off to sleep that night I recalled the names of 13 YHA members from Melbourne that I knew were in London or the UK at the same time as me. All of these, including myself, were members of YHA during the period 1946 to 1953. Those were exciting years, when the club had its own bus and we were building a YHA ski hostel on Mt Buller. All were skiers, with whom I had skied during those wonderful years. Now, here we were in London, testing out our self reliance, and seeing how the other half lived on the other side of the world. During the writing of this book, I realised that there were five more YHA members of the Buller group in London at the time, making a total of 17 (Leon had already gone back to Australia). In no particular order, they are as follows;

Gil Rowe, Joan Cooper, Rosemary Roberts, Leon Langley, Netta Higgins, Elizabeth Loughnan, Maurice Spanger, Lionel Kane, Bruce Norman, June Lucas, Judy McMillan, Lin Coughlan, Len Clarkeson, Gwen Greensill, Betty Nutting, Betty Whitelaw and myself, Gordon Smith.

My daughter Virginia, I am proud to say, followed in her father's footsteps not once, but twice, in 1977 and 1980.

Saturday 18th April 1953: In the morning I looked at a few more boarding houses, but none were as good as number 22 with Ma Banks. After dinner I went to the Palais. It was crowded with Scots after the soccer game that had been played at Wembley. I met a couple of Irish girls, but they were hopeless, complaining about this and that.

Sunday 19th April 1953: This was the day we put our clocks forward one hour for 'daylight saving time.' It was a lovely sunny day, so I decided to go for a walk around London. I got off the bus at Piccadilly Circus and walked down the Strand past Australia House and along Fleet Street. Then along Cannon Street past St Paul's Cathedral, which I vowed to visit some time later. Finally I came upon the historic Tower of London and Tower Bridge that crosses the Thames in the London Docks area, adjacent to the Tower.

The Tower Bridge is a majestic engineering structure with its two high towers and drawbridge. It was built in 1894. The machinery to raise the drawbridge was driven by steam engines, which were replaced by electric motors in 1975. Then I saw the movie *The Cruel Sea* in the West End, which starred Jack Hawkins, but I thought that there was nothing outstanding about the movie.

Chapter 17
A MAGICAL NIGHT AT THE BALLET WITH THE WIVES

Monday 20th April 1953: My mother wrote to tell me that Mrs. Clarke, a Great War widow and neighbour of ours at Rosanna, was in London. My mother included Mrs. Clarke's phone number in her letter. We only saw Mrs. Clarke every now and again, because she managed a guest house on Phillip Island. I rang Mrs. Clarke, who was thrilled to hear from me. We made a date to get together on Thursday night. After dinner I decided to go to the Palais to see what it was like there on a Monday night. Ted Heath and his jive band were playing and I actually jived a bit with an Irish girl; but true to form she was a complaining type, just like the other Irish girls I have met at the Palais.

Tuesday 21st April 1953: As we had planned at Easter, I met Ralph, Sheila and Jean in the foyer of The Royal Opera House. Sheila and Jean looked particularly beautiful in their smart dresses. We made our way up the staircase because for this performance, we would be watching the ballet from a box. We were directed to our box by the usher. It was really quite exciting as we moved into the overhanging box and took our seats. The stage was so close that we could make out small markings on the stage boards. This was the first occasion that any of us had been in a box, let alone one in the Royal Opera House. Our box was on the first tier. There are three tiers.

I well remember my first visit to the Royal Opera House, when I was enchanted by the huge, Royal Burgundy colour of the stage curtains, with the large Royal coat of arms embroided in gold on the drape that stretched from one side of the stage to the other. The curtains had ladder-like, gold borders extending the full height of the curtains and across the bottom, with Royal insignias at the lower corners of the curtains. I never ever tired of seeing them and the thrill of watching them part, to reveal the beginning of a performance.

Together with the two lovely ladies, Sheila, Jean and my mate Ralph, this was to be a most exciting night. One of the best I was to spend at the ballet. The first ballet we saw was the *Ballet Imperial*, set in Russia at the time of the Czars, however, at the time I thought it was all about the upcoming Coronation. The principal dancer was Rowena Jackson. The theme music was Tchaikovsky's Piano Concerto No 2, sometimes used as the name for this ballet. I purchased the record of this concerto, which I like much better than the more popular Tchaikovsky Piano Concerto No 1. This was followed by *Swan Lake* with Alicia Markova. The final ballet, *Tiresias*, I had not heard of before. Margot Fonteyn was the principal dancer in this fantastic ballet, which takes place in Crete with lots of athleticism, sensual movements and copulating snakes. It was really a turn on, a sexually, exciting ballet with Fonteyn dancing superbly.

The view from the box was definitely one sided. I felt that it was nearly possible to reach out and touch the dancers. The squeaks and other noises made by their feet could be heard sometimes, which was a bit of a pity. We were conscious too, that people in the stalls and other seats in the theatre, are always interested to see what celebrities were sitting in the boxes. They would have been disappointed just seeing us, although Jean and Sheila were certainly worth looking at.

Even though I have not mentioned many of their names, the male dancers such as Brian Shaw, John Field, Phillip Chatfield, Alexander Grant, Frederick Ashton and Michael Somes were amazing to see. Quite apart from their dancing ability, I am quite sure they must all be among the best athletes in the world.

After the show we went around to the stage door where we handed over our programs to an attendant who took them for signing to Margot Fonteyn and Frederick Ashton's rooms. We had quite a wait before we got them back. While we were waiting, Jim and Brian came along in the car to pick up their wives. This was quite embarrassing; because they were shouting out insulting remarks to us about the ballet, and about us wanting ballerina's autographs, much to the amusement of all the other fans waiting with us.

At last, our programs were returned with Frederick Ashton's and Margo Fonteyn's autographs. We kissed the girls good night and waved to them as they were whisked back to Stevenage in Jim's car, while we made our way back to our lodgings. It was a wonderful night. Sadly, I no longer have any of my autographed programs, but that is another story.

Thursday 23rd April 1953: As arranged, I met Mrs. Clarke at the Regent Palace Hotel. It was wonderful to see her. She hadn't changed much, she still had her rather masculine, booming voice. I reckoned she must be nearly 70 years of age or older. We talked for hours about ourselves, what we were doing, what we had done, what Rosanna was like since I left. She was very interested in my visit to the Isle of Wight, and how I had compared the island to our

Phillip Island. I suggested that she should make time to visit there and like me, compare the town of Cowes, with the Phillip Island Cowes. It was a great reunion, so very enjoyable to be meeting each other in London of all places. Before leaving me Mrs. Clarke gave me her address in Russell Square. She was about to go on a bus tour around the Continent, and would be back in London only between 29th May and 3rd June for the Coronation. When I left the hotel I was immediately accosted by a beautifully dressed prostitute. I thought from the manner in which she was dressed she would have been rather expensive.

Friday 24th April 1953: I wrote to my mother about my meeting with Mrs. Clarke. I watched a great show on TV with the BBC Dance Band, *Showboat,* which has lovely theme tunes for the opening and closing of the show.

Saturday 25th April 1953: I bought some records at HMV in Oxford Street. In the evening after dinner, I was off to my usual haunt, the Hammersmith Palais. Surprise, surprise! Who should I meet there, but Ralph's wife Gladys with a boyfriend. She looked a little guilty, but she had no need to. I had a quick thought that I might ask Gladys for a date, but decided not to. It would have been only to try and glean some information to give Ralph about her activities, and maybe giving Ralph some grounds for divorce as he encouraged me to do. I had a dance with Gladys, talking small talk as we danced together.

That visit to the Palais I suppose you could say, was part of the social life of a Londoner, I danced with a number of young ladies with diverse personalities. One of those with a short hairdo, gave me the 'come hither look,' but nothing came of it, she was just a bit of a tease. Her blonde girl friend however, taught me a little more about the art of jive. I had a dance with a slightly older, attractive lady, who I enjoyed talking with about music. She was a cut above the others and didn't chew gam. I actually made a point of not dancing with any gum chewing girl.

Sunday 26th April 1953: I woke up very late and went into the West End. London was like an open book to me now. I was truly a Londoner. It was very exciting to be in London at this time, a lot of flowers were beginning to bloom and the trees in the parks were sprouting green leaves. Not only were the signs of spring on show, but there was also decorations and structures being built in readiness for the Coronation. I went to the cinema to see *The Final Test*, another new release. It starred Jack Warner and Robert Morley. It was a very topical movie, seeing that the cricket tests were not far away. The movie was about a top batsman who was devastated when he found out that his son wanted to be a poet and not a cricketer. I then wandered through Soho before I caught the bus home.

Chapter 18
A *COMET* CRASHES AND THE AFTERMATH

Tuesday 28th April 1953: I stayed home and watched TV instead of going to the YCA. I was fascinated by the announcers who read out the weather reports each night on both radio and TV, especially when they mentioned Cape Finisterre. It sounded very mysterious, quite apart from bringing back memories of my life on board the *Moreton Bay*. All the BBC announcers have beautiful speaking voices and accents, or should I say lack of accents, they just speak perfect English.

Wednesday 29th April 1953: I met Ralph at Covent Garden, but nearly didn't make it. There was a big traffic jam at Walham Green, because Chelsea was playing their last match of the season at their football ground nearby. We saw the ballet *Der Rosenkavalier*, which was quite good with many dancers on the stage most of the time. The ballet music was composed by three of the great Austrian composers Johan Strauss II, Franz Lehar and Richard Strauss, so of course I enjoyed the music very much.

Afterwards, we had a couple of nice Carlesberg Pilsners at a pub near the theatre. I suggested we drank Carlesberg, just to honour my visit to Carlesberg's factory in Copenhagen. It was a nice drop, but expensive. I told Ralph that I had seen Gladys with a bloke at the Palais, and that I had a dance with her. He was 'all ears' and thanked me for telling him. "Good on you mate." Ralph took me home in the car, which had just been repaired. We were attempting to get seats to the ballet for Coronation Eve, but weren't having much luck, because we had left it too late to book.

Friday 1st May 1953: May Day. I watched the TV, but did not see any May Day processions. I wrote a letter to May, once again just keeping her and her family up to date with what I was doing in London.

Saturday 2nd May 1953: Terrible, terrible news on the TV and radio, about a *Comet* that had broken up after take-off from Calcutta, with the loss of 43 passengers and crew. The cause of this loss was found to be the failure of an elevator spar. Despite this tragedy, *Comet*s continued to fly. Strangely, from hearing the *Comet*s overhead during the night last month, I had not heard any since. This was the first of a series of accidents involving loss of life when *Comet*s broke up on take-off, the cause of which was determined and overcome. Then in 1954 another *Comet* broke up in mid-air, the cause unknown. All the *Comet*s were again grounded. The remaining *Comet*s underwent a stringent examination to find the cause of the disasters. A *Comet* fuselage, was continuously stress and fatigue tested in a water tank, until eventually a crack was detected. The crack began in the corner of a window and spread, eventually resulting in structural failure and the break-up of the fuselage. This was deemed to be without doubt, the cause of the *Comet*s breaking up in flight.

The *Comet*s were then modified and went through years of redesign, to become a very successful, long haul, pressurised aircraft, operated by many aircraft companies around the world. The last *Comet* flew for revenue in 1973. One *Comet* has since been preserved and there are hopes that it will be able to fly again.

I shopped in Putney and came home to watch the soccer cup final between Blackpool and the Bolton Wanderers. Blackpool was the victor, 4 goals to 3. The Queen was at the game looking beautiful as usual. I went to the Palais in the evening, where I danced with Noreen, one of the girls I had danced with the previous week. We got on very well, but during the evening she told me she had TB and a collapsed lung! I didn't know what to say or do, but I was very attracted to her. She gave me her phone number.

Sunday 3rd May 1953: I woke up late to a superb day. After I finished lunch, I wandered through Hyde Park and heard various religious and communist, soap box orators, all spruiking about nearly everything. Some were worth listening to. I thought I had missed the May Day procession on Friday, but as I walked down toward Piccadilly I came across the May Day march, a few days late. I watched as it passed through Trafalgar Square, along the same route as last year. The banners were very interesting. 'Youth for Peace and Socialism,' 'Get rid of the Yanks' and 'Communist Party Holborn,' were some of the more prominent ones.

When I returned to number 22 for lunch, Len Clarkeson rang and invited me to come and spend the afternoon and evening at his flat. I got a very pleasant surprise to see Gwen Greensil and Elizabeth Loughnan there. It was great to see them both again. Afterwards we all went to a local pub, where we sank a few beers and talked madly about what we had been doing.

On the way back home in the tube, I got a terrible fright because I thought I was on a runaway train! On both occasions when I had visited Len, I hadn't really noticed much about my tube journey on the Northern Line out to Hampstead. The train was going at an enormous speed. This always looks so at any time in the tube, because you can only see the sides of the tunnel through the windows. The train went around corners, up and down, passed one station without stopping, then another. I definitely thought the train was out of control, and to make matters worse, I was the only person in the carriage. I was very scared. Thankfully the train stopped at the next station, Camden Town. I hadn't noticed that the train ran express through Belsize Park and Chalk Farm.

    I thoroughly enjoyed travelling on the Underground, a wonderful system. It is quite easy to get to know the system with the help of a little card map supplied by London Transport. For the usual places I travelled to on the tube, I knew my way around quite well. Some of the curiosities of travelling on the Underground are quite interesting. Standing on the platform, before the lights of the train can be seen in the tunnel a strong rush of air occurs, as there is only a very small clearance between the train and the tunnel sides. This is caused by the train pushing a column of air in front of it, acting like a piston in the 3.65 m (12 ft) diameter tunnels,

    It was also fascinating, when sitting in the carriage as the train sped along, which it really does, to look through the glass doors at the end of the carriage into the next carriage. It is like being on a roller coaster ride on some of the lines, as the train went around curves, moved up and down, apparently dodging sewers, water mains and the like. The Underground, in its present form of third rail, electrically driven trains, first began running in 1890. There was roughly 160 km of underground line at the time I was in London, making an interconnected system of eight routes. Each of which, are named, Piccadilly, Bakerloo, Northern and Central lines, giving some hint of the areas of London that each of these lines serves. With its trains, people, its escalators, lifts, subways, advertising boards and signage, the Underground was for me 'The Wonderland of London.'

Chapter 19
A DAY AT THE BEACH WITH THE YCA

Monday 4th May 1953: There was wonderful news for me when I got home from work. I had secured a seat in a grandstand for the coronation, which I had booked through Australia House.

Tuesday 5th May 1953: I went to the YCA in the evening and helped canvass votes for the Conservative Party. I took Corinne home and as always, she was dressed beautifully, but regrettably, she has no personality. Becoming a member of the Young Conservatives gave me the opportunity to meet many young people of about my age, but maybe, with rather different views than mine, regarding politics. It would not have surprised me, if some of the members didn't give a damn about politics, but were more interested in its social activities and the opposite sex. Of course I was too, but the YCA offered me more than that. I learnt a lot about local government and many other aspects of how London worked. The YCA for me, was also a substitute for YHA.

I was very surprised that not once since I joined the YCA, had I heard any criticism of the Labour Party. If there had been, I think I might have left, but the members were a great bunch of young people with very open minds, not at all like Mr. and Mrs. Baker and Ma, who were so fond of criticising the Labour Party. With regard to me going round the neighbourhood giving out leaflets to entice people to vote for the Conservative Party (Tory) in a local election, I had no guilty conscience then, or as I look back. Why? Because, I was in fact, campaigning for a man in a Tory by-election in Churchill's, party. Winston Churchill became Prime Minister again in 1951 when the Conservatives won the election. If however, I had been asked to campaign for Margaret Thatcher, who became Prime Minister in 1979, I am sure I would have made some excuse to decline, or maybe I would never have joined the YCA in the first place, The Labour Party did not regain power until 1964 under Harold Wilson.

Wednesday 6th May 1953: In the evening I met Ralph and we went around to the nurse's flat to see about Ralph's Coronation seats, which the girls were getting for him. Ralph got his seat for the Coronation and some of the girls had also got their seats, so we were all very excited. There wasn't much going on there, so Ralph and I retired to our favourite pub, the Crew's Quarters at the Star and Garter where we sank a few pints. Ralph told me that I had been instrumental in bringing an end to his relationship with Gladys, when. I told him that I had met Gladys looking very guilty, with a bloke at the Hammersmith Palais the other night. He said how glad he was that I had seen the pair and told him, because he was following up on their relationship with the possibility of filing for divorce.

Thursday 7th May 1953: There was much to interest me on the TV this night. Preparations for the upcoming Coronation, the cricket tests, and John Hunt's expedition attempting to climb Mt Everest.

Saturday 9th May 1953: I went to Australia House to confirm my booking for the seat at the Coronation. Then I did some shopping as I needed a few things for my trip to Littlehampton the next day with the YCA. In the afternoon I watched TV and went to the cinema in Putney where I saw *The Yellow Balloon* starring Kenneth Moor and Andrew Ray. It was a good drama, but nothing special.

Sunday 10th May 1953: I was up early and off to join the other YCA members on board a coach in Putney. I got quite a shock by the way they were all dressed. They looked as though they were going to the ballet at Covent Garden, not to the beach at Littlehampton. They all wore suits with ties and the girls were quite formally dressed too. I looked very much out of place. I wore 'formal beach clothes,' my fawn slacks and open neck shirt and my new light blue jumper.

Littlehampton is 190 km from London on the south coast of England in West Sussex, halfway between Bognor Regis and Worthing. It was a great ride in the coach with all the YCA members on a lovely, sunny day. The coach went through Guildford and Arundal. The countryside looked so beautiful and colourful as the coach travelled along, passing houses with extensive, well kept gardens where most of the flowers were in bloom.

When we arrived at the Littlehampton beach, although the sun was out, there was a cold wind, so none of us went in for a swim. I found Littlehampton to be a pleasant seaside resort with a wide, yellowish, sandy beach. We lazed on the beach and remarkably, I got a little sunburnt. Instead of swimming, it was decided to play a game of rounders, or was it baseball? I was not sure which and I don't think anyone else knew either. Believe it or not, all the blokes put down their good suit coats to use as bases, but I kept my jumper on. Although the activities were a little different than a day on the beach in Aussie-land, it was great fun and I enjoyed every minute of the day. The coach stopped briefly at a pub on the way home for a few cooling beers, or should I say room temperature beers, but that is part of life in England. The day ended with me tired, but happy. The cost for the day was 8/6 each, for the coach.

I learned later that the beach town of Littlehampton was where Anita Roddick was born in 1942. Anita was the lady who founded the Body Shop. She married Gordon Roddick and together they started up the company. The first Body Shop was opened in 1976. At the time of writing, the company has 1,000 shops in 40 countries, with its headquarters in Littlehampton. The cosmetic products sold in Body Shops, are only derived from environmental friendly sources and practices.

Monday 11th May 1953: As I had promised when I saw Betty Nutting at the party, I took Betty to the Hammersmith Palais, where we danced to Victor Sylvester's band. Like me, she had danced many times to his band on records. It was a great thrill for her to be able to dance to the real band. We had a pleasant night, dancing very well together. Between dances, we talked about everything we had both done since leaving Australia and everything we expected to do, before going back home.

Betty left Melbourne on the *RMS Orcades* in September 1952. In February 1953 she travelled through France, Italy and Austria, skiing for 12 days in Lech. She went via Switzerland and France back to London, where she worked in the city as a stenographer at A W Bain and Sons insurance brokers. Betty spent Easter in Holland. After the Coronation, she intended to hitchhike around the Continent staying at youth hostels. She planned to visit the Scandinavian countries, then Belgium, Luxembourg, Germany, Switzerland, and France, before returning to London. Later in the year, Betty planned to tour through Scotland and Wales. We had a great night together, parting with a wish to see each other again.

Tuesday 12th May 1953: After dinner, I don't know why, but I rang Noreen, the girl with a collapsed lung. I went to Sudbury Lane where she lived. I think curiosity was my motive for this date. We walked around Wembley and then went to a pub. Noreen was a Catholic, certainly not my type, as I thought when I first met her. When I took her home, I met her father and brother and evaded the question of making another date. Besides, I was not sure if a collapsed lung was actually TB, and was contagious?

Wednesday 13th May 1953: Ralph came over and told me that our grandstand seats were all together, including Gladys's seat. Ralph did not want to sit with Gladys at the Coronation, so he rang John, a friend of his, who took her seat. With that arranged we went over to the nurses' flat, to see about getting another seat for Gladys from the nurses, who were looking after an allocation of tickets from Australia House. I was happy now that Ralph had got rid of Gladys, especially as I had played a small part in it.

Friday 15th May 1953: Pay day again. I had an efficiency of 176%. I was earning very good money at Bridges lately, sometimes nearly £8 for the week, so I was able to put a little aside each week for my next and last tour.

Saturday 16th May 1953: I was told at work that there was a good dance on at the Astoria Dance Hall in Charing Cross. I decided to forsake the Palais and go along. It was quite a good dance band, playing old time and modern dances. There were a lot of Aussie sailors there; because there were a few warships in port for the Coronation. I decided I wouldn't go there again as the Palais was much better. Besides at the Palais, I don't think there were any Aussies there except me.

I picked up a free copy of a folder, put out jointly by London

Transport, British Railways and the Metropolitan Police, titled; *Elizabeth R Coronation*, which I still have in my possession. It listed all the arrangements for the buses and railways in London on Coronation Day. It unfolded to show a large, coloured map, of the route for the Coronation procession, which the Queen chose herself.

The Queen would leave Buckingham Palace travel along The Mall, then into Northumberland Avenue, along the Victoria Embankment, which has been reserved for children. She would then go by Bridge Street and Parliament Square into Westminster Abbey. After she had been crowned, she would leave the Abbey and travel along Whitehall, Cockspur Street, Pall Mall, St. James Street and along Piccadilly to Hyde Park Corner, where it will turn into the East Carriage Road to Marble Arch, then turn right, into Oxford Street, Regent Street, Haymarket, Cockspur Street and back along The Mall to Buckingham Palace. I can't wait!

Sunday 17th May 1953: I went into the West End to have a look at my grandstand seat. Most of the grandstands had been erected and the decorations put up all over London. They consisted of placards of crowns, lions, and unicorns hung above the route, together with garlands strung across many streets. I found my seat without too much trouble. It was opposite Hyde Park, on the East Carriage Road, which runs parallel with Park Lane. The seat was about 200 m from Hyde Park Corner, towards Marble Arch, about halfway between the two. The procession would move from our left to our right along the East Carriage Road, Our seats were only about 80 m away from the centre of the road, so we should have an excellent view of the procession.

I was very pleased with what I had seen. Then I went to a matinee at Covent Garden and saw *Giselle*, which was really beaut.

The May Day procession in London

YCA Members all dressed ready to go to the beach

The floral garlands across Brompton Road

The author relaxing on the beach at Littlehampton

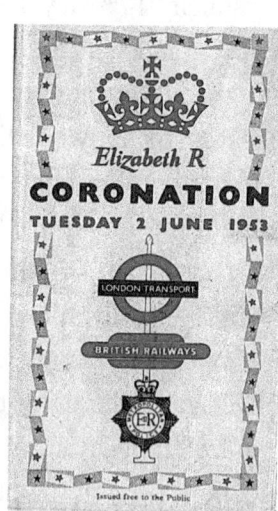

The Coronation information folder cover page

The principal dancers were Alicia Markova and Anton Dolin. After the ballet I saw the movie *Citizen Kane* with Orson Welles and Joseph Cotton. It was a very interesting movie and was the first time I had seen one about the newspaper industry. I was by myself for the whole day. It was very pleasing to be free to go where I pleased without any compromises.

Tuesday 19th May 1953: I had been receiving some birthday cards in the post for a few days, because it was **MY BIRTHDAY TODAY.** I am 26 years of age! Ralph rang to say that there was a problem with the Coronation seats. We were invited out to see June Lucas on Thursday night, to sort it all out. In the evening I went to YCA where we had a dance night, dancing to records, which wasn't too bad. Except for the letters I got, the day was just like any other of my days as a Londoner. In fact I think it was a lot quieter and I had no complaint with that.

Wednesday 20th May 1953: I went to Frank's house again, the UYCA bloke. He had invited Mrs. De La Monte, a councillor to speak about the local Borough Council, which was quite interesting, another notch in my knowledge of local government. I took Corinne home again. If only she had some vivacity. Maybe it was my fault: I should challenge myself to bring it out of her, because apart from that I enjoyed being with her. I supposed this was because of the aura of her job with *Harper's Bazaar*, although I have always been an admirer of elegantly dressed women. She obviously enjoyed my company and thinking about it later, I should have kept dating her. One never knows, she may have introduced me to the social life of fashion journalists

Thursday 21st May 1953: Ralph and I went to June Lucas's for tea and met all her Aussie friends there, Joachim, Bob, Caroline and Charlie, but none of them were YHA members. I wasn't sure where they fitted into the picture. They were a nondescript lot, who didn't impress Ralph or me very much at all. We all ended up at The Denmark, a pub very popular with the Aussies who inhabited the 'Kangaroo Valley ghetto.' The Denmark pub also did not impress us. In fact it made me very glad that I had kept away from the social life of the Aussies in Earl's Court. Around 11 p.m. Ralph drove us all back to number 22, where I played some of my records for a short while. We did not have any drinks of any kind and were fairly quiet.

After they had gone, I had a ding-dong row with Ma, who objected to me bringing my friends (some weren't, I must say) back to my room. Bugger her! Then I found a note on my bed saying that Netta was back in London and to call her. This made me very happy because I missed her a lot.

Chapter 20
I GET A CALL FROM MY MOTHER

Friday 22nd May 1953: Netta rang. It was so pleasing to hear her voice again. I invited her to come with Ralph and me to the Star and Garter. She said that would be nice. I rang and asked Ralph to pick her up. We enjoyed our drinks with Netta. She told us all about her tour of Austria, where she had skied on a glacier, and then her tour around Germany. We finished up in my room until Ma chucked us out at midnight, but not before we had all arranged to go up to Stevenage for the weekend. Netta collected her skis and the case I had picked up for her from Victoria Station. It was wonderful to have Netta nearby again.

Saturday 23rd May 1953: I went into the West End shopping and when I came back home, Ma said there was an urgent, telephone call, from Rosanna for me. Ma had taken the call, but said it wasn't very clear. I was worried, wondering what the problem was, hoping that my parents and two brothers were OK. What to do? I waited all the afternoon for the call and at 6 p.m., then I put in a call to the cable office, but with no result. I left Sheila and Brian's phone number at the cable office, and went and I met Ralph and Netta as arranged at King's Cross and told them about the message I had received. They were very concerned for my sake.

We drove up to Stevenage, where we met Sheila and Brian at

The Unicorn in Stevenage. I introduced Netta, whom they had heard a lot about from me. We had a drink and then retired to Sheila's to sleep. I told Sheila and Brian about the message, and warned them that they might get a phone call in the night. Like the others, they were a little worried for my sake. I tried to forget all about it and enjoy this day at the beach with my friends.

Sunday 24th May 1953: We were off for a day at the beach at Clacton, but there was no phone call before we left. The drive was around 100 km through Colchester. Once again it was a beaut drive through the English, spring countryside. Arriving at Clackton-on-Sea, I admired this very popular, English, seaside resort in Essex on the south coast of England. Clacton has a long pier as well as a wide, sandy beach and the large township is full of guest houses, hotels and amusement places. We met Jean and Jim at Clacton and spent a lovely day on the beach. I went for a swim with the blokes, but the water was very cold.

At last Netta met all of my friends, who on so many occasions I had told her how wonderful they all were. We spent the day relaxing on the beach and had a snack lunch at a beach food stall. At the end of a pleasant, sunny day, Ralph was going to drive us part of the way back to London. Late afternoon, Netta and I wished everyone goodbye and thanked Brian and Sheila for having us.

Ralph drove home through Colchester and as arranged, let Netta and me off at Romford about 20 km from London, so that he could cut across country to Stevenage; because he was staying with Sheila and Brian for a few more days. Ralph said we could catch a train, but we decided to try and hitch a ride. Many cars passed us, but none stopped. We both had our rucksacks with just a few overnight things in them, so we looked like genuine backpackers. Around 10 p.m. we gave up and decided to hop on an all-night 291 bus service, which operated throughout Greater London. Although I had a great time, I didn't think Netta enjoyed the weekend much, although she thought my English friends were great. I got back to number 22 at 2.30 a.m., after seeing Netta home. Ma said that there had been no phone call from home. I went to bed, still rather concerned.

Monday 25th May 1953: I booked a call for Australia early in the morning and then went to work. Today was the Whitsun Holiday, but Bridges only permitted a half-day holiday, so I was home for lunch. It was a lovely hot, 28°C day, but I had to stay home waiting for a call. Nothing at all came through before I went to bed. I imagined the atmospheric conditions must have been bad, or the original call was a false alarm.

Tuesday 26th May 1953: I rang through to check on the call, but again nothing. After work, I waited for the call before going to a dance at the YCA. I took Corinne home again, because I was madly attracted to the beautiful way she dressed, but other than that she had nothing, or maybe it was me that was the problem. I still couldn't animate her, although she still seemed happy being in my company.

Wednesday 27th May 1953: At last at 6.15 a.m., I finally got through to my mother and we talked for 10 minutes. She didn't sound very happy at all, but I need not have worried, everyone was well, but missing me. It was a relief to know that everything was all right with my family. I hardly recognised my mother's Aussie accent, as her voice was 'very working class Australian,' from Collingwood if I could put it that way. She sounded very sad, just like she had looked the night I sailed. I wondered if she had been sad ever since I left. I hoped not.

The reason for the call, which had given me so much worry,

was that my Uncle Reg wanted me to buy a racing car crash helmet and gloves, all expenses paid. I was to take a day off, buy them and air-mail them to him. The total cost of the phone call was £10. I decided to take the day off to buy the helmet and gloves, but first of all I rang Bridges and told them that I wouldn't be in and gave the foreman a vague idea of what I had to do.

I looked up the business pages of the phone book and found a motor racing accessory shop not far from Parson's Green. I wasn't at all sure, when I had bought the helmet and driving gloves, how the hell I was going to pack and mail them back to Australia. More to the point, how much it was going to cost? However, one thing at a time, I rang the company and explained what I needed. They said they had racing helmets and gloves in stock. I said I was a little concerned about the cost. The salesman said not to worry. The company would package them and post them COD, which was the way they did a lot of their business. That was a great relief.

I went out to the shop, where the salesman was most helpful choosing the helmet and gloves for me. I was surprised at how easy the purchase was with hardly any trouble at all, except to supply the address of my father and sign a form or two. The transaction was over in less than 30 minutes. I hoped that the items I selected were OK. The total cost came out at around £40, and that was via air-mail.

Regarding the phone call from my mother, there was no comparison with the trouble I had trying to make contact with my mother in Australia in 1953, to the ease with which communications had advanced in 50 years. On Christmas Day in 2001 I rang May, who was married and living in Ireland. Having sought out the correct exchange numbers, I simply dialed the number and 'hey presto,' I was immediately talking to her and wishing her a Merry Christmas and Happy New Year. Besides it was very cheap.

Having successfully completed the purchase of the helmet and gloves, it was just past noon, so instead of going back to work, I went into the West End to have another look at the Coronation decorations. In Oxford Street Selfridges had constructed a huge Coronation presentation on the front of the store, with the Queen riding on her horse; it was a fantastic display. I just couldn't wait for Coronation Day to come around. The excitement was beginning to build up.

My Uncle Reg had taken up motor car racing during the 1956 Olympic Games in Melbourne. He took part in the Australian Grand Prix on a course around Albert Park Lake. He drove a Cooper-Bristol, racing against Stirling Moss, an English champion motor car-racing driver of the time. My Uncle Reg was a very dynamic person. He had initially started up a radio business called Smith's Radio and also set up one of the first used car yards in Australia, which he called Reno Auto Sales, with the slogan 'Divorce Your Car at Reno.' He got most of his ideas from flying over to America and seeing how things were being done over there. Sadly on the evening of 2nd October 1960, when I was married and living in the Australian Alps, I received a phone call from my father, telling me that my Uncle Reg had been killed in a car race on the Mount Panorama racing circuit, at Bathurst. He was driving a Porsche, when on a long straight the car became airborne, left the track and hit a tree, killing my uncle instantly. He was 57 years of age.

Chapter 21
CORONATION EVE AND SAINT PAULS CATHEDRAL

Thursday 28th May 1953: After dinner there was panic for a while at number 22 because the TV had broken down! Now of all times, but Ma was up to the challenge. She took steps to have it repaired straight away, and this time she didn't blame me as she was prone to do on some other occasions when the TV faltered. The fault most times was that a valve had 'given up the ghost.'

Friday 29th May 1953: After work, I had my usual bath, this time, to be nice and clean for the Coronation. I wrote a few letters before I went off to bed.

Saturday 30th May 1953: In the afternoon I went in to the West End to see more of the Coronation stands and decorations. London was very busy as there were a lot of people from outside the UK here for the festivities. I had a surprise phone call from Betty Whitelaw, another Buller YHA member who I heard was also in London, with her mother in tow. She had been given my phone number by one of the other members. She asked if I would like to come with her and her mother to visit William Shakespeare's Playhouse next Monday, the day before the Coronation. I said, "Yes I will look forward to that," so we made arrangements to meet on the day.

June Lucas rang and invited me to a party at the flat. Off I went, but there were only a few nurses there and they were all just sitting around. I had brought a bottle of Stingo beer with me, but other than that there was nothing to drink or eat. After drinking my Stingo, I excused myself and left. I decided to walk into the West End and see all the decorations lighting up as it got dark. Joan Cooper wasn't there. If she had been I would have taken her with me. It was a lovely balmy evening as I passed Hyde Park Corner and began walking along Piccadilly, where I was accosted by 'ladies of the evening' every 50 m or so along the way. The first one was by Park Lane and wanted £3. I must admit I was tempted, but thought better of it. As I walked further along past Mayfair, the price dropped to £2 and so did the standard of the girls. The price kept dropping as I crossed Piccadilly Circus. In Shaftsbury Avenue the price went rock bottom. "A quick one for 2 bob mister?" Presumably in a doorway. Needless to say that was the end of the quotes.

Walking around a little more I discovered the Daybreak Jazz Club in Soho, where I had a really good time dancing to a noisy, but good band. After a while, I called it a day and went home to number 22 on an all-night bus, finally tumbling into bed at 5 a.m. It was all great fun.

Sunday 31st May 1953: I didn't get up until nearly noon, which was not surprising. I had read in *What's On In London* about conducted tours of Battersea Power Station, and having seen the huge building across the river on so many occasions, I decided to go and have a look. I joined a tour, which I thoroughly enjoyed. Real time working exhibits are far more interesting than museums.

Battersea Power Station has actually two coal fired, power stations, 'A' and 'B', which in 1953, were combined to form one large station that generated 509 MW. We were first conducted through 'A' station built in 1933. It generated 400 MW and was designed by Sir Giles Scott, who also designed Waterloo Bridge and the ubiquitous, red telephone box. We were then escorted through station 'B' of 109 MW capacity. The construction of this power station began just after the end of World War II and began generating this year 1953. 'A' power station was much more aesthetically decorated in its interior, with parquet floors, a marble turbine hall and wrought iron staircases, whereas the more modern station 'B' had a much more utilitarian interior.

Sad to say, in 1983 Battersea Power Station was closed down. It had been running only on 'B' station since 1975. Various attempts were made since it was closed down to preserve the historic buildings, all manner of ideas having been put forward on how best to use the facility. As I write Battersea Power Station is owned by Malaysian investors and is being gradually redeveloped into a huge complex of shops, offices, restaurants, bars and open spaces. When complete it will have 250 residential units as well as many entertainment facilities. At the time of writing, the first section is complete and occupied. It was my hope is that the power station would not be demolished, so I am happy with these developments and long as the iconic chimneys are left in place, which is assured, because the power station was declared a heritage site in 1980.

Unbeknown to me at the time, when I returned to Australia, I worked for ten years on the Kiewa Hydro-Electric Scheme in Victoria and have written a couple of books on its construction. One book is titled: *Working and Raising a Family on the Kiewa Scheme 1953-1963 Second edition.*

Monday 1st June 1953: It was a showery day when I met Betty Whitelaw and her mother, a charming, middle aged lady. I hadn't seen Betty since we skied on Mount Buller a couple of seasons ago.

Clacton on Sea

The author on the beach at Clacton with the mob L to R Jean, Jim, Ralph, Sheila, Brian and Netta below right

Selfidges Coronation display in Oxford Street

Reginald Hillard Smith

Battersea Power Station

The three of us went first to see William Shakespeare's Playhouse The Globe, at the address shown on our map, but there was nothing there except a memorial plaque. It was a bit of a disappointment, especially for Mrs. Whitelaw.

We then walked along Fleet Street admiring the lovely decorations high above the street, festooned with flowers and flags, stretching from one side of the street to the other. Soon we came to St Paul's Cathedral, with its huge dome. I can still remember the classic photograph of St Paul's Cathedral we saw during the war, with the dome standing out defiantly, against a backdrop of smoke and flames.

St Paul's Cathedral was designed by Sir Christopher Wren. He was asked by Charles II in 1675, to build a cathedral on the site of the former church ruins. St Paul's Cathedral was the result, being completed in 1710. The dome rises 110 m above the ground and is 34 m in diameter. The 'Whispering Gallery' that I had heard about in school was most intriguing.

We tried it out and it really worked. The phenomenon of the 'Whispering Gallery' and its acoustics is a function of the perfectly circular dome, beginning about halfway up the interior of the circular wall that supports the dome. Mrs. Whitelaw, Betty and I, took turns to station ourselves on opposite sides of the gallery and whisper each other's names, hard up against the wall. We were amazed that our words could be heard clearly on the opposite side, after travelling 54 m around half the circumference of the gallery, an amazing phenomenon!

St Paul's is typically Gothic in architectural style, with north and south transepts. I found the interior to be relatively plain, compared to many churches I have seen, but looking up from below into the dome was awesome. It is a massive cathedral. To compare St Pauls to a mountain as is my wont, was not easy, but I chose Mt Blanc, the highest mountain in Europe, as its mountain counterpart, huge but not beautiful. I thoroughly enjoyed the outing with Betty and her mother and wished them a great day for the Coronation.

Many years later, Tom Webb told me that Betty and Neal Fitzgerald another YHA member who I knew well, were about to become engaged. Betty's mother did not approve, because she was C of E and Neil was a Roman Catholic. Mrs. Whitelaw decided to take Betty abroad in an attempt to sever the relationship with Neal because mixed marriages were frowned upon in those days. Mrs. Whitelaw's plan didn't work however, because some months after they returned to Australia, Betty and Neal married and lived happily ever after.

Chapter 22
THE QUEEN'S CORONATION AND EVEREST CLIMBED

Tuesday 2 June: **CORONATION DAY.** I rose a little later than I had intended and gulped down my breakfast. Exciting and spectacular as I knew the day was going to be, it began for me, in a totally unexpected and marvellous way. As I walked toward Fulham Road to catch a number 14 bus to take me to my reserved seat in the grandstand, I saw a paperboy holding up a copy of the *Daily Express* with a banner headline that read, **'ALL THIS AND EVEREST TOO.'** I bought a paper and was thrilled to read the reports that Mt Everest had just been climbed by the New Zealander Edmund Hillary and his Sherpa, Tenzing Norgay. The news was a wonderful present for the Queen on her Coronation Day.

The credit for getting the news of the climb to London in time for the Coronation, went to James Morris a member of the expedition, who was high up on the mountain in the Western Cwm. He set out immediately to walk to Kathmandu, from where he was able to get a message through to London with the great news. The timing was perfect, but coincidental.

Since I was a young lad, I have read many books about mountaineering, many of them about attempts to climb Mt Everest, especially those by Frank S. Smythe, who in 1933 from Tibet, climbed higher on Everest than anyone up to that time. I was probably just as excited by this news as by the fact that this was Coronation Day and I would soon be seeing the Coronation procession.

I found my seat in the grandstand in the East Carriage Drive stand by 7.30 a.m. and not long after I was joined by Ralph and his friend John. It was going to be a long wait before the procession began. There were a couple of heavy showers early in the morning, but our spirits were not dampened, as we were well rugged up. Directly behind our seat there was a large temporary stand, put up by the BBC for radio and television commentary.

It would have been great to have had a modern, small, portable radio so we could have heard what they were saying, but they were yet to be invented. There were stalls behind the stands where we could purchase drinks and food, so while we waited we ate and drank. Too many for me, as it turned out. We talked to the people around us about ourselves, themselves and where we came from. Most were Canadian and Australians. We waited patiently in exciting anticipation of what was to enfold before us.

Later in the morning the weather cleared up a little and at 11 a.m., a buzz went through the stands. We were told that the Queen had just left Buckingham Palace and was on her way to Westminster Abbey. The BBC commentators in the TV stand were keeping the people close by, informed of what was happening. This was being relayed to the people in our stand and other grandstands close by. While we were waiting for the news that she had left Westminster Abbey, there were light intermittent rain showers.

Eventually, about 2.30 p.m. we heard that the Queen had left Westminster Abbey and the procession was on its way. I made sure my camera was ready, and I had a new roll of film unpacked and handy to put in the camera when I had taken the first eight shots. It was a good half-hour, before we heard cheers coming from the direction of Hyde Park Corner. The excitement around us escalated as the cheers gradually grew louder, until at last we spotted the golden coach in the distance, unfortunately not shining in the sun, because there wasn't any. However, nothing could dull the opulence of the golden coach, flanked by the Yeomen of the Guard in their brilliant red and gold coats, breeches, and black peaked caps. The horses too were brilliantly decorated.

At last the procession was upon us and what a show it was. That coach, wow! In a matter of moments the golden coach had passed us by, but I saw the Queen clearly with the crown on her head, because luckily she was on our side of the coach. I took a couple photos as the procession approached and when the golden coach with the Queen passed in front of us.

The long, colourful procession that followed, was made up of the armies, air forces and navies of the Commonwealth countries and their bands. Of course we cheered our Australian marchers the loudest of all. At one point there was a short holdup in the procession. As luck would have it, the Royal Canadian Mounted Police were halted directly in front of us for about two minutes. Their uniforms were a brilliant red, a much brighter red than I had seen in photographs and the movies. As luck would have it too, it gave me a chance to change over the film in the camera.

The procession took just under an hour to pass us by. It was a magnificent spectacle seeing the Queen in her gold coach and then the members of the armed forces of all the Commonwealth nations marching past with their bands. Just after the Queen passed by, I asked Ralph to take a photograph of the procession, with me holding up the front page of the *Daily Express,* showing the headline about Everest.

After the procession came to an end, nearly everyone from the stands spilled out onto the East Carriageway Road. Ralph, John and I walked along to Marble Arch and Oxford Street where we caught the tube to Hampstead, in order to get the best view of the flyover of about 20 aircraft which was fantastic as they emitted red white and blue smoke. Having enjoyed the seeing the flyover that didn't last very long, we then went to a café to get something to eat, but I didn't feel hungry.

After we said goodbye to John, Ralph picked up his car and we drove to the nurse's flat, but I felt crook, so Ralph took me home. After I got into my room, I had to rush out to the toilet. I was violently ill, and collapsed into bed. That was the rather sad conclusion to a unique and exciting day. The only part of the Coronation celebrations that I regretted missing, was the fireworks display at night. The day had been just too long and exciting for me, but I wouldn't have missed it for worlds. I didn't write up my diary and notebook of the wonderful Coronation Day until the following morning.

The television coverage of the Coronation was a unique event in many ways, especially the televising of the ceremony in Westminster Abbey. When the question of televising the ceremony was raised by the BBC, there was much opposition, especially by the clergy and the nobility. This was because an ancient rite decreed that only they, should be present at the ceremony. However, the Queen thought otherwise. After much thought and advice, she decreed that the ceremony should be televised, because she wanted as many of her subjects as possible to witness the event.

This was the first time that TV cameras were allowed inside Westminster Abbey. There was only one stipulation, there were to be no close ups. It was estimated that the ceremony in the Abbey was viewed by 53% of the population of the UK. As there were only 2.7 million TV licences issued, each TV set must have been watched by multiple viewers, and it was thought that about 20 million people were able to watch the ceremony on the small black and white screens.

Luckily Ma Banks had her TV repaired before the day. As an example of the multiple viewing, she had at least 10 people in the room with her to watch the event; Gwyn and Sylvia, Barbara and Chris, Brian, Auntie Maude, Mr. and Mrs. Cornish, to name a few. The wireless coverage went around the world. My family would have been listening to it back in Australia. There was no TV in Australia until just prior to the Olympic Games in Melbourne, in 1956.

Wednesday 3rd June 1953: I felt sick at work all day, although I finished the day OK. Í watched replays of the Coronation ceremony in Westminster Abbey on the TV. I rang Winnie Clarke to see if she had had a good day. She did, saying she had an absolutely, wonderful day, one that she would never forget.

Thursday 4th June 1953: I saw more replays of the Coronation on the TV and was looking forward to the next big event in my life. Leaving England on my next tour on the way back home. I was in no hurry for this to begin, as I was still enjoying my life as a Londoner and had many more things to do and see.

Friday 5th June 1953: My work efficiency was 110 %, but I had to fight for it again. I was convinced that now, the time had come when I must look for another job. After work I got a ring from Ralph to meet him in Golders Green at the Bull and Bush pub, so off I went. After a few drinks there we went to The Spaniards, a night club.

Although I have been to many pubs in England, I don't think I

John left and the author waiting patiently in the grandstand

The BBC broadcasting booth just behind our seats

The Queen's Coach approaching

The Queen's coach as it passed by directly in front of us

The procession passing by after the Queen's carriage

The front page Of the *Daily Express* with the procession in the background

ever went to one that wasn't a joy to be in and drink their beer, even if it was at room temperature. The Spaniards however, didn't have that ambience. After paying a small fee we left and Ralph took me home. I learned later that Dickens wrote about The Spaniards in *Pickwick Papers* and Keats wrote *The Ode to A Nightingale* there.

Sunday 7th June 1953: After dinner I went out to Nellie's and saw Netta. We exchanged experiences of our day at the Coronation. Netta didn't have a grandstand seat, but watched the procession from amidst the crowd. I said to Netta. "I bet that if it was the Pope who was being crowned, you would have made sure you had a grandstand seat." Surprise, surprise, my remark didn't go over very well. A movie of *The Beggars Opera* was showing in a cinema in the West End. I wanted to see the movie, but sadly Netta wasn't interested in coming with me, even though I had told her all about my experiences with *The Beggars Opera.*

I left Netta and Nellie and went into the West End. The movie starred Laurence Olivier as MacHeath and Stanley Holloway as Mr. Peacham. The movie was a John Gay version. The songs and storyline were a little different from the Brecht and Weill opera, but still quite enjoyable. This was the fourth version I had seen of the opera: I reckoned I was quite an authority on the opera by now.

After the movie and because it was such a lovely balmy evening, I decided to walk down to Trafalgar Square through Admiralty Arch and along the kilometre long Mall, past the Queen Victoria Memorial to Buckingham Palace. The wide, bitumen surface of The Mall is an unusual, pinky-purple colour, and its approach to the Palace is simply out of this world, so dramatic.

Chapter 23
CHANGING JOBS, FRANK SINATRA AND SYLVIA

Monday 8th June 1953: I finally made the decision this morning to look for a new job. Although the pay at Bridges wasn't too bad, the working conditions were poor and I had to fight for my bonus nearly each week. A local newspaper had an advertisement for a tradesman 'marker off' with English Electric Napier and Sons in Acton, not far away from Putney and near where Pamela lived. I took the day off and went by trolley bus along Fulham Palace Road, through Hammersmith past the Hammersmith Palais and on to Acton, a total distance of some 4 km.

I walked through the door of the large two story factory and was directed to an office where I was interviewed by the employment officer. The first question he asked was, "How long I will you be staying in London?" He explained that the company was not employing any more Australians, unless they intended staying with the company for at least six months. I was about to tell him I would be in England for only another two months, however, I quickly recalled the lesson I had learnt at Kings, and decided to keep my future plans to myself. I said, "If I like the job I will be here for longer than six months." This seemed to satisfy him and he said I could start on Wednesday. The pay was the same as Bridges without the bonus. I wouldn't have to get up any earlier, Napiers began work half an hour later and finished later, and that was no problem.

Again I tried to find a new house with full board, but they were either too small, not full board, or too expensive, so I decided to stay at number 22 for the last two months. I would just have to reconcile myself to the fact that I couldn't have any girls in my room, which was really a saviour for me anyway. Netta was the only girl Ma let me take up to my room by myself. What that said about Netta, or me for that matter, I was not quite sure.

I finished off a very busy day going to the Wembley Empire Pool an annexe of the famous, iconic, Wembley Stadium. I went there to see the Harlem Globtrotters and the All Stars. Two American teams that play basketball and travel around the world giving demonstrations of their basketball skills. The basketball game I saw was very fast, skilful and enjoyable, but not as good as Aussie Rules football, might I say. However, for me the highlight was a long demonstration of the fabulous way they can manipulate the ball. They also showed us some very funny comedy routines using their superb, ball handling tricks that they could do with the ball. It was a great show.

Tuesday 9th June 1953: I put my notice in at Bridges and collected a small amount of cash. They wished me well, but didn't say they were sorry to see me go. In the evening I went to the YCA where an English chap gave us a lecture about Australia. He talked about many aspects of Australia, the government, the cities and the climate. I thought he did a fair job, but I didn't let on that I was an Aussie, neither did anyone else tell him, which I thought was a bit strange. I thought someone in the club was sure to introduce me to him, but no one did. On second thoughts, it may have embarrassed him. I heard that Sylvia had parted with the bloke she was going around with. I thought I might ask her for a date sometime, but really I was silly, I should have kept dating Corrine.

Wednesday 10th June 1953: My first day on my new job at Napiers. I travelled by double decker trolley bus, a very quiet means of transport compared to the diesel buses. The trolley bus went along Fulham Palace Road to Acton, from where I had a short walk to Napiers. It was a pleasant change of working conditions from Bridges. I had a locker and the canteen was large and served good food. Ma had made me jam sandwiches for work each day at Bridges, but I didn't tell her there was no need to any more.

The name of my employer was Napier and Sons of Acton. Napiers were a manufacturer of motor and aero engines and were closely associated with English Electric, well known for its electrical products of all types. In conjunction with Napiers, however, the accent was on aircraft. The English Electric, *Canberra* jet bomber, the first British jet bomber to serve with the RAF, was a famous product of the company.

My new job as a 'marker off' was easy and clean. It entailed marking or scribing lines on aluminium castings, to indicate to a machinist where to remove metal from the casting. I worked at a large, cast steel table with a very flat surface, on which I mounted and secured the casting to be marked. With reference to a blueprint or drawing of the casting, and by the use of various measuring and marking gauges, I scribed lines, arcs and circles for the guidance of the machinist. The scribed lines showed up quite clearly, because I first painted the general area where the lines would be with white marking paint. It was a good worthwhile job.

Friday 12th June 1953: Today at lunch time I wandered around the factory. I didn't see any old dilapidated machines, but I did see many machines I had never seen before, such as an automatic gear-generating machine, a much more modern machine for making gear wheels than I had operated in the railways.

My job as a marker off was a tradesman's job, because a knowledge of geometry and the use of vernier measuring instruments was necessary. That is one of the many skills a tradesman fitter and turner learns to do in his apprenticeship. The ability to read engineering drawings and blueprints was essential too. It was not the type of work that a 'dilutee' could do. From what I had seen of the work at Napiers, I doubted if there were many dilutees employed in this factory, such as at Kings.

Saturday 13th June 1953: I shopped in the West End and went to my bank, finding I had £50 in my account. That amount, together with some pounds I kept with me, should I reckoned, be enough to see me across France, down into Italy and back home. I came home and watched the third day of the Test at Trent Bridge on the TV. The Aussies were getting thrashed, Bedser taking 7 for 55! I went to the Palais at night and got on marvellously with an Irish girl, one that didn't complain about everything. But I didn't get her phone number or make a date.

Sunday 14th June 1953: I went to see Sylvia in the morning to ask if she would like to come to see Frank Sinatra in Putney that night, a solo performance at the local theatre. She readily agreed, so after dinner I picked her up and off we went to see the great man. We took our seats and the lights were lowered as Frank Sinatra, small in stature, walked out onto the stage with a chair. The audience applauded loudly. He was unaccompanied, except for a pianist. Sinatra sat down on the chair and lit a cigarette. Then without further ado he began to sing his favourite song, 'Nancy with the Smiling Face.' Without waiting for applause, he went straight into the next song, after which he sat in the chair and called out to the audience. "What do you want me to sing now?" Everybody yelled out the names of songs. He pointed to one person and asked for their request?

For the next hour and a half, except for a pause every now and again to wait for the applause to die down and to light another cigarette, he sang all the songs the audience requested, some of them twice. I was amazed at Sinatra's energy and ability to sing for so long. Sylvia and I were thrilled to have seen this famous person in real life and hear him singing. Afterwards we played records at Sylvia's place until about 12 15 a.m. It was good to be with her again. I thought that I might be happy dating her until I leave for home and not to worry about Corinne any more. I regretted however, that I had not invited Corrine to come to the ballet with me.

Chapter 24
THE BALLET, WEEKENDS IN STEVENAGE AND TV

Tuesday 16th June 1953: The Test match at Trent Bridge ended in a draw because it was rained out the day before. I went to the YCA and took Sylvia home, so it looked as though we were together again.

Wednesday 17th June 1953: Pay day at Napiers, but of course I didn't get much. The castings I was marking off were for a jet powered helicopter. The jet engine, I was told was inboard, the fan-jet air being delivered to the rotor blade tips, causing the blades to rotate. When I returned to Australia I was not able to find out the fate of the helicopter. I can only assume that it never got into production. Maybe this was because of problems with sealing and directing the air flow out to the blade tips, however this is pure assumption on my part, until I learn otherwise. In the evening I took Sylvia pub crawling and then we went back to her place. Her mother was out and we kissed on the couch, but without the passion that was there when I first took her out

Saturday 20th June 1953: I told Ma Banks I had changed jobs, and not long after, Ma told me that she wanted her weekends to herself. I told her that Sylvia and Barbara had talked to me about this a week ago. I said I had no problem with her request. She thanked me and we left it at that. I didn't object because on many occasions I was away for the weekends. Ma Banks left the Corn Flakes for me for breakfast. For dinner if I wasn't away, I usually went to a café nearby for a cheap meal.

I shopped in the West End and rang the taxation office and enquired about my taxation, telling them I had changed jobs and would be leaving the country in August. They said I was not eligible for a rebate; because I would not have worked a full year in the UK. I just hoped they used my tax money well.

I met Ralph in the evening and we drove up to Stevenage, where we met the mob and went pub crawling to Welwyn and Hertford. Pub crawling consisted of drinking first at one pub, then after a few drinks, the next pub to drink at was nominated. The last car to get there bought the drinks, the first round anyway. That night we drank at three different pubs. It was quite a hazardous exercise, with the three cars, the Hillman, Morris Oxford, and the Ford Consul tearing along narrow country lanes in an effort to be first to the next pub. This was the new, hazardous pastime they had dreamed up while I was living in London..

Sunday 21st June 1953: We played records and then went to the Crooked Billet for a few beers. After that we drove to Jim's place in Hitchin for a lovely dinner. We had a game of tennis in the afternoon on full stomachs, which needless to say did not produce very good tennis. Back to Brian and Sheila's for our evening meal, then to a pub in Stevenage, until it was time for me to catch the bus home. Surprisingly, I had a little money to spare, so this time I travelled back to London in luxury on the train. I wondered how many Aussie backpackers were leading the same exciting, sometimes hazardous social life that I was involved in. But then again, I am a Londoner.

Monday 22nd June 1953: I was really enjoying my work days at

Napiers, even the ride to work in the trolley bus each day was beaut. Amongst many letters I received was one from my mother saying that Tommy Handley had been killed in a car accident. He was my grandmother Griffin's son-in-law and was married to Melva, her adopted daughter. They had been married for six years and had a daughter and son. I had only met Tommy a few times. I selected a bereavement card and sent it with a letter to my parents, as I didn't know Melva's address.

After dinner I met Ralph at the Soho Casino where we saw *Tom Arnold's Review* with Cicely Courtneidge. The performance was rather punk, except for a song called 'Pussycat.' I listened to Cicely Courtnidge on the radio many times back in Australia, laughing madly at her comedy routines. She was one of England's outstanding comedians. However, in this show at 60 years of age, (she was born in 1893) she was just not the comedian that I remembered listening to some years ago.

Thursday 25th June 1953: I watched a little of the first day of the second Test from Lords, then after tea I took some of my records around to Sylvia's place. It was a hot night. After we had played a few records her mother went out, and the night got even hotter when we had a very intimate time on the divan. I wasn't sure who was trying to seduce who, but the inevitable mutual seduction happened. It was very gratifying and exciting for us both. I remembered my scout motto. 'Be Prepared,' and I was. As I was leaving, Sylvia gave me another attractive photo of herself. I thought that our relationship together, was more mature now. I was excited to be with Sylvia again. That was really the reason I dropped dating Corrine, beautiful clothes are OK, but they have no intrinsic emotions. I left Sylvia's house around 1 a.m. a happy Aussie backpacking Londoner! It was a very dark night, and I was carrying a heavy bag with all my records in it.

As I walked along I was confronted by two men. 'This is it, I am gone'! I thought, because there had been quite a few 'muggings' locally. Then one of the men asked me, "What have you got in your bag?" "Records" I shakily replied. He said "Don't be alarmed, we are plain clothes policemen." One showed me his badge and said that they were just checking, as there had been some bad types around the area lately. He asked me, "Could I have a look in your bag please?" I showed him the records. "Thank you very much, sir," he said and off they went. I was never very good at quick repartee, but I wished later that I had replied. 'That's all right cobber' in my best Australian accent. They certainly gave me a hell of a fright until I found out who they were.

Friday 26th June 1953: I had a letter from Harry Gilliam, a Rover Scout friend who wrote that he might see me in London, when the Rover Scout moot they were attending in Austria finished. I watched the Test on TV again.

Saturday 27th June 1953: In the morning I went into the West End to confirm the taxation requirements prior to me leaving the UK. There were none. I fed the pigeons in Trafalgar Square, thousands of them, and then went home. In the evening Netta and I went to Convent Garden, where we sat in my usual two, forth row seats in the stalls.

We saw the ballet *Veniniana* with Violetta Elvin, then *The Shadow* with Svetlana Beriosova. She danced very gracefully and apart from her dancing ability, I think she was my favourite ballerina. She is a blonde, whereas most of the other ballerinas are brunettes. Frederick Ashton's *Homage to the Queen* with Phillip Chatfield and Rosemary Lindsay was the next ballet, first performed on Coronation night. The ballet was designed not only to honour Queen Elizabeth II, but to showcase all the leading ballet dancers, male and female, together with the corps de ballet. It was a most thrilling extravaganza.

We also saw a very famous person from the ballet world that night, when Dame Ninette de Valois came on stage for the final curtain call. It was a tribute to her outstanding career as a ballerina, teacher and choreographer, and her important role in starting up the Sadler's Wells Ballet Company in 1947. It was a wonderful, wonderful, night. It was also full of highlights because we 'rubbed shoulders' with another famous person.

More correctly, it was me that did the 'shoulder rubbing' when Netta and I went out to the bar at the interval, and I purchased our drinks. When I brought them back to Netta, she was very excited, saying to me "Did you see who you were standing next to at the bar? Quick, take a look!" I turned around and saw a large man in a dinner suit by the bar, next to where I had been standing. I immediately recognised him as Netta excitedly exclaimed "It's Gregory Peck!" I didn't think I had ever seen Netta look so radiant. Gregory Peck is very tall and looked exactly as he does on the screen.

There was an enigma about that fantastic night at the ballet. I copied the spelling of the ballet *Veniniana*, exactly as I had written it down in my diary. However, I could not find a ballet of this name in any ballet reference books. Without my program to refer to, (because they were stolen), I am at a loss to know exactly which ballet it was we saw, danced by Violetta Elvin.

Sunday 28th June 1953: In the afternoon Netta and I went to see a movie, *Viennese Waltzes*, which was most enjoyable, then we strolled around the West End. We didn't talk much. Netta has her moods. I suppose I have moods too. I think we both probably realised that we were nearing the end of our stay here in the UK, and if it wasn't for a difference of religion, there might have been a future for us together.

Tuesday 30th June 1953: I had been watching the Test cricket on the TV for the last couple of days, but this one ended in a draw. Thank God for an exciting game like our Aussie Rules football. I went to YCA and took Sylvia home. With many kisses we parted, but not before we had made a date to see each other again.

Friday 3rd July 1953: On the TV I was thrilled to see some films of the Everest expedition. A large plaster model was used to show all the various routes up Mt Everest, including the final successful route. It was very enthralling television. The original unsuccessful attempts to climb Mt Everest were made through Tibet, along the Rongbuk Glacier, up onto the North Col and the north-east ridge. Tibet later closed its borders to climbers, but climbers were permitted to approach Mt Everest through Nepal.

In 1952 a route was found up the Khumbu Ice Fall and the Western Cwm to the South Col by a Swiss expedition, but the expedition failed to reach the summit of Everest. This was the same route taken by John Hunt's successful expedition this year in 1953, which Hillary and Tenzing took to reach the 8.848 m (29,028 ft) summit of Everest on the 29th June. They climbed up the icefall and the Cwm to the South Col, and from there on to the summit.

I will never forgive the Chinese for their invasion and desecration of Tibet in 1950, and particularly for reducing to ruins the Rongbuk Monastery, beside the East Rongbuk Glacier, in full view of magnificent Mt Everest. I cannot comprehend, how any so-called human being could carry out such an act of vandalism with Mt Everest; (Chomolungma, 'Goddess Mother of the World') looking on in the background. To my thinking the Chinese invasion of Tibet, the massacre of the Tibetan people, the destruction of their culture, together with the destruction of their monasteries and temples, was as brutal and just as much a crime against humanity, as the Nazi holocaust.

Saturday 4th July 1953: I met Ralph at his new dental practice in North London and off we went to Stevenage for the weekend. After dinner at Sheila's we went to a pub in Hitchin for a few beers, then around 10 p.m. there was a big fireworks display in the Priory Grounds. It was a really spectacular show, but did not make up for the one I missed on Coronation Day.

Sunday 5th July 1953: I sunbaked all morning in the glorious sun. Although the weather in London has been very hot, there was never really, a clear, blue sky in England, just a light, hazy blue. As I sunbathed, I remembered what a summer's day was like back home, where the clouds on a hot sunny day were fleecy wool cumulus, which became more widespread during the day. I also missed seeing my mountains the Dandenongs, the Healesville and Warburton Ranges. The fields in summer in England still remained green, quite unlike the fields and paddocks back home, which in summer changed to dry, brown nearly everywhere.

In the afternoon we went up to Letchworth and had an enjoyable round of golf. Later Sheila and Brian broke the news that they were going to have a baby, so we all had a drink to celebrate. It was then time for me to catch the train back to London, after another exciting weekend in Stevenage amongst my English friends. With going up to Stevenage and all the other things going on, it was no trouble for me that Ma Banks wanted Saturdays and Sundays to herself.

Monday 6th July 1953: A welcome letter from home told me that my parents had deposited another £40 in my bank to make sure

I had enough to see me home, my mother's idea, I was sure. I would now have £90 at least for my tour through France and Italy to Naples and the voyage home, although, just another £40 I would be in debt. I was beginning to think that £50 odd, was really going to limit my backpacking tour through France and Italy, as well as on the ship back to Australia, but now thanks to my family, I have no worry in this regard.

Tuesday 7th July 1953: In the evening I went to The Boathouse with Sylvia, where we had an enjoyable drink together. When I took her home and after we kissed goodnight, like a fool, I told her that in just over a month, I would be leaving for Australia, but it didn't seem to make much of an impression on her.

Chapter 25
NETTA LEAVES RETURNS TO AUSTRALIA

Wednesday 8th July 1953: After dinner Ralph and Pam, who looked quite beautiful, picked me up in the Consul. Then we picked up Netta and Nellie and went to Dirty Dicks, a pub in Bishopsgate in the City area of London. Dirty Dicks was opened in 1870. It got its name from a person who lived there. When his fiancé died, he said he would never wash again.

The interior of Dirty Dicks was certainly not like a normal pub. Everything inside, the chairs, tables and walls, were roughly styled, giving a dirty appearance, but in reality, it was quite clean. The waitresses were dressed in old fashioned skirts and bonnets, which surprisingly enhanced the atmosphere of the restaurant. This occasion was to say goodbye to Netta and wish her Bon Voyage. Sadly, it would be the last time I would be seeing her until I returned to Australia. We had a very enjoyable time at the pub, but I forgot to ask Netta what ship she was sailing on. Netta was a special friend to me in London. I first got to know Netta when we skied together with YHA on Mt Buller and Mt Baw Baw although we were not close friends, and it was a great surprise when she met Leon and me on Waterloo Station on our arrival in London.

As we skied together for two weeks in Grindelwald, a bond between us grew because we found we had so many other common interests, especially the ballet and theatre. There was however, always a huge religious barrier between us, which prevented our relationship being anything other than Platonic. I was critical of Netta on many occasions and she of me, but this never harmed the affection we had for each other.

When I returned to Australia, Netta and I dated on a number of occasions. The last was when I invited her to come down and stay at my parent's holiday house by the beach in Mordialloc. In the evening we went for a walk along the beach. After talking at length about our relationship, we came to the sad, but mutual conclusion that there was no future for us together. The last time I saw Netta, was when I took her to the railway station and with a hug and a kiss, she boarded the train.

After being fired in late October 1953 from the first job I had back home, mainly because I didn't like the job and couldn't concentrate (ship lag I suspected), I found a marvelous job with the SEC Kiewa Hydro Hydro-Electric Scheme at Mt Beauty. When I married in 1955, I sadly lost all contact with Netta. In 1997 my wife Dilys and I were invited to attend the 50 year anniversary of the opening of the YHA Hostel on Mt Buller, which Netta and I helped to build, before going abroad. I was eagerly looking forward to meeting Netta, but she was not present. I was told that she had died of a brain tumour many years previously.

I was deeply saddened and shocked. Nobody at the reunion could tell me any more about Netta and neither could other YHA members back in Melbourne. Eventually in 2004 I resorted to the births and deaths register on the Internet, where I discovered that Netta died in 1973, only 50 years of age. I also discovered that after she returned from the UK, Netta joined the Melbourne University Ski Club and was the club's treasurer for a number of years before her death. Netta never married. This brought to a sorrowful closure my relationship with a very dear friend, but not quite.

There is a sequel to our story. Around 2004 I had a phone call from Netta's relations, brother and sister. They had been browsing the internet and saw my name. I had published some of my books as **Smashwords Ebooks**, and as a consequence, they can be accessed on the internet together with my name as the author, which is where the contact was made. They phoned me to see if I was Netta's friend. I assured them I was. We met, and as can be imagined, we talked extensively about our lives, but in particular of course about Netta. It was an exciting and somewhat sad reunion, during which, I was told that I was the only man in Netta's life.

Chapter 26
TO THE BALLET AT THE ROYAL FESTIVAL HALL

Thursday 9th July 1953: The Australians were 3 for 120 on the first day of the third Test at Old Trafford, but I didn't think by the way they were playing that they had any hope of winning.

Saturday 11th July 1953: I had a terrific argument with Ma in the morning because I forgot to tell her I would be away for the weekend. I didn't think I had to, because she was no longer cooking for me at weekends. I met Ralph in the West End and we drove up to Hitchin on a lovely sunny day. After lunch we played tennis, had a drink at the Crooked Billet and then walked to Sheila's, where as usual we had a very, succulent lunch.

Sunday 12th July 1953: It rained all morning, so again we drank at the Crooked Billet and played dart cricket, the English (Brian) against the Aussies (Ralph and me). Sorry to say the English won. After lunch, Mrs. Day, Brian's mother and I played a very pleasurable game of golf at Letchworth, until we got rained off the course. I returned to London again by train, after another enjoyable weekend with my friends. Even though I had lent my golf clubs to Ralph, I never really tried to see if there were any suitable golf courses near Putney, where I could go and have an occasional round. Judging by the few enquiries I made, the London district clubs were mostly private and exclusive, so I decided to forget about playing golf while I was living in London.

Tuesday 14th July 1953: I watched in horror as our Aussie batsmen went out for ducks galore on the last day of the Test. The result was another draw. It's as bad as soccer with draws this time however, because two days had been rain affected. I went to YCA, but excused myself and came home early to see the Everest Expedition on the TV. I saw John Hunt, the leader of the expedition, very English, Tenzing Norgay, the charming Sherpa porter with a beautiful smile and of course Edmund Hillary. It was so wonderful to hear his New Zealand accent and see his boyish smile and easy manner. Also on the TV were Bourdillon and other members of the expedition. The expedition members introduced and described a film and photographs of the successful climb. It was really exciting television.

Wednesday 15th July 1953: After dinner on a lovely balmy evening, I made my way to the ballet, this time not to Covent Garden, but to the Royal Festival Hall on the south bank of the Thames. As I crossed the Hungerford railway bridge, I could not help but admire the city skyline beyond Waterloo Bridge. St Paul's looked as I always imagined it should, dominating its surroundings.

Festival Hall is a large modern style building, built in 1951 as part of the Festival of Britain, the idea of the Labour Government to commemorate the centenary of the Great Exhibition of 1851. It was also intended to show the world that the UK was well on the way to re-establishing itself as a world leader in manufacturing and technology, after the end of World War II.

The site chosen for the Festival was on the south bank of the Thames, between Westminster and Waterloo bridges, a rather derelict area improved immensely by the Festival buildings. The Royal Festival Hall is a big, slab sided building with a low curved roof. The side that faces the Thames has huge plate glass windows, but the building itself is architecturally quite plain. The concert hall inside is able to seat 3,000 people and the acoustics are excellent, with much design thought having been given to this aspect of its construction. The Royal Festival Hall is also sound proofed from external noise, as Waterloo Railway Station is directly behind the hall..

During the interval I walked into the glass walled art gallery, which overlooks the Thames River. Night had fallen over London revealing a magnificent view across the Thames. The view was absolutely magical. A floodlit Big Ben and a new moon over Westminster Bridge in a dark leaden sky, were all reflected brilliantly in the shimmering water of the Thames.

The ballet performances that night were some of the most enjoyable I have seen. I regret that I do not have the programs to refer to, only my diary entry notes of the day and my memory. The ballets I saw were *Les Sylphides*, *Alice in Wonderland*, an exciting picturesque ballet and a new modern ballet, *Symphony for Fun*. I loved its kaleidoscope of Tin Pan Alley music. The Royal Festival Ballet was created by Alicia Markova and Anton Dolin. Markova did not dance, but I believe it was Anton Dolin I saw in *Les Sylphides*. This, I think, was the fourth time I had seen this classical ballet, each production being a little different. It was a magical night!

Chapter 27
EXPLORING BOURNEMOUTH WITH PAM

Saturday 18th July 1953: I went into the West End and shopped, buying a pair of shoes and a shirt. I also went around the various tour agencies, picking up travel brochures for France and Italy. I would soon have to plan my route to take me across France and Italy and on to Naples to catch the *Orion* home.

I took the tube out to Ralph's surgery in Finsbury Park. We drove up to Hitchin on a lovely fine day. In the afternoon we had a game of tennis with the girls. Then after tea we went up to the Brewhouse Inn, where I vowed to drink sensibly because I wanted to enjoy the occasion, which I reckoned would probably be the last time I drank at this wonderful convivial inn, where I had spent so many enjoyable hours with all my English friends, the mob.

Sunday 19th July 1953: We loafed around in the morning, then late afternoon I played a horrible 18 holes of golf at Letchworth with Mrs. Jones and Brian. Afterwards we had a few drinks at a local pub. Then it was time to say goodbye and this time catch the bus back to London.

Tuesday 21st July 1953: I went to the YCA and got the 'brush off' from Sylvia. The same thing had happened with Marie at Stevenage. I should not have told Sylvia I would be leaving for Australia, until the last few days. Once again I was too honest. I didn't blame Marie or Sylvia for wiping me off, because there was obviously no future for them with me, nor had there ever been. I was reading *Lorna Doone*, which I found especially interesting seeing I had visited the part of the country that is the background for the book.

Thursday 23rd July 1953: Ralph and I went to the Palladium to see the American singer Guy Mitchell, a favourite of mine. I was thrilled when he sang 'She wears red feathers' and a few of my other favourites. Although Guy Mitchell had the large Palladium orchestra accompanying him, his show was in many ways a disappointment. His voice and the songs he sang were quite melodious, but his performance was not up the Frank Sinatra show I had seen with Sylvia at the small local theatre in Putney. Guy Mitchell seemed to have a set repertoire of songs that he and his orchestra were going to perform, whether his audience liked them or not! When people in the audience called out songs they wanted him to sing, he completely ignored them.

Friday 24th July 1953: I had heard so much about Bournemouth, which is supposed to be one of England's premier beach resorts. I decided to go and see for myself if it was true. I rang up Pam, Netta's friend from South Africa and invited her to come with me next Sunday. If Sylvia hadn't given me 'the brush' I would have asked her, but why- oh- why didn't I invite Corrine to come with me? I really don't know.

Saturday 25th July 1953: I went into the West End on a glorious day and paid the balance of my voyage ticket of £30/15 with money I had saved and put aside for just this purpose. The total cost of the voyage was £80/15. I confirmed that the sailing date of the *Orion* from Naples on Friday 18th September 1953 was unchanged.

.Sunday 26th July 1953: I met Pam at Gloucester Road and we went by bus to Waterloo Station where we caught the train. The fast electric train passed through Southampton, where we saw the beautiful liner *Queen Mary* in the distance. Then on to Bournemouth 166 km from London, in Dorset on Poole Bay. I found Bournemouth to be quite a beautiful beach resort. There was a large jetty with a pavilion at its end. Although the beach was wide and quite long, the sand and the water was not a very attractive colour. The town has many parks and gardens, all with beautiful flower displays, which we admired. There were many hotels, guest houses and shops to cater for the tourists. I was particularly struck by how all the houses in the town were so very neat and tidy.

We talked and walked all day, finishing up at a restaurant where we had a few beers and enjoyed a lovely meal. My overall impression of Bournemouth was of a lovely, seaside town, so when my English friends extolled its virtues, I could now agree with them. Bournemouth was also well known for its very good symphony orchestra. We had a few beers in the train's pub carriage on the way back to London, and finished up having supper (a high tea) at Pam's. She said she enjoyed the day and so did I.

Tuesday 28th July 1953: I was thoroughly enjoying my work at Napiers and was very sorry I hadn't left Bridges a couple of months earlier, when I had my first problems there. I was sorry too that I would be leaving the company in three weeks' time. I watched some of the final day of the fourth Test at Headingly on the TV, very disappointed and annoyed it was another draw. I was very pleased however, with the manner in which BBC TV combined the cricket with the Children's Hour. They continued to show the Test play virtually without interruption, but all the commentary was directed at the children. They showed and named the fielding positions, and the cameras zoomed in to show the bowler's grip on the ball, the batsman's stance and how he gripped the bat. They also showed the score board, explaining the meanings of all the numbers. It was really instructive. I learned a lot about the game myself. I went to YCA, but came home early as I was feeling tired.

Thursday 30th July 1953: There was a good opera on the TV, so as Ma Banks didn't mind a bit of opera, I stayed in and watched it with her. It was Mozart's *Die Entfuhrung Aus Dem Serail* (*The Abduction from the Harem*). The production came from Glyndebourne. I was aware that Glyndebourne is an opera venue in Lewes in Sussex, 86 km south of London. Every year it stages the Glyndebourne Opera Festival, which is one of the great cultural events of the year. The opera company began there in 1934 in an old mansion, but now a modern opera house has been constructed, capable of holding an audience of 1,200 people.

The opera I saw on TV was one staged during this festival. This was the first time I had seen this great opera. Even seeing it on a small, black and white TV screen, did not diminish my enjoyment of the opera. The story of the opera is really fully explained by the title, *The Abduction from the Harem.* The major characters are Osmin, the basso profundo overseer of the harem, and the wonderful soprano voice of Constanze, a beautiful captive and favourite of the Pasha's harem. All of the cast were great actors and singers. The whole opera was filled with excellent voices, humour and drama. Although the opera was sung and spoken in German, it was accompanied with subtitles. It was a very exciting opera.

In later years I became more familiar with the opera, when I purchased a record of Sir Thomas Beecham, the famous English conductor in a rehearsal of *Die Entfuhrung Aus Dem Serail*. The unique experience of hearing a rehearsal was absolutely fascinating, especially with some of the humorous comments made by Sir Thomas.

Saturday 1st August 1953: When I went to the Royal Festival Hall last month and on the way crossed over the Hungerford Bridge, I didn't have my camera with me. It was such a fantastic view of London from the bridge that I decided to go and take a few photos of the view along the Thames that I saw on that occasion. Today was ideal weather, so off I went and managed to get a great series of photos.

Chapter 28
WINDSOR CASTLE AND A THAMES RIVER CRUISE

Sunday 2nd August 1953: I rang Pam and invited her to come with me to visit Windsor Castle. She said "She would love to." We took a bus to Windsor 34 km from London. Windsor Castle, with its two circular turrets can be seen from quite a long way off, because the castle stands on a rise above the town of Windsor.

We joined a guided tour of the castle. Windsor was the third castle that I had been conducted through on a guided tour, Schonbrunn Castle in Vienna and the ruins of Heidelberg Castle. Schonbrunn Castle however, cannot be compared with Windsor Castle, which has the distinction of being the largest, inhabited castle, in the world. Schonbrunn Castle is well past its use as a residence for kings and queens, but certainly not for tourists.

Windsor Castle is a particular favourite of Queen Elizabeth II who, we were told enjoyed spending weekends there. The interior of the two castles are very different. Schonbrunn with its wide variety of lavishly, decorated rooms, compared to the more sombre interior of Windsor Castle. The building of Windsor Castle was begun in the 13th century by William the Conqueror and since then it has been continually modified and extended.

The rooms inside the castle are very large and beautifully furnished. The walls are lined with many works of art including portraits of kings, queens and famous people. The dining and ballroom in particular are magnificently decorated, but of course we did not see the private accommodation where the Queen stays when she is in residence.

We had a stroll around outside the castle through its lovely, green gardens, containing many beds of beautiful flowers. The park and grounds of Windsor Castle are huge and well laid out seeming to stretch away for miles, covering a much larger area than those of Schonbrunn. Strolling through the gardens were some of the Queen's Grenadier Guards, resplendent in their beautifully tailored uniforms and large fuzzy hats.

Leaving Windsor Castle, we walked into the rather small township of Windsor, its shops overflowing with souvenirs of the castle. We had a refreshing drink at a pub and a bite to eat, after which we took the train back to London, finishing up at the Boathouse. Pam was great company and we got on well together.

Monday 3rd August 1953: Bank Holiday. I was so glad the weather was fine, because I decided to go for a boat cruise down the Thames to Margate on the edge of the North Sea. When I got on board the cruise ship the *Thames Maiden*, I discovered there was a BBC film crew on board, making a documentary of the cruise. There was also a BBC helicopter hovering above us from time to time, no doubt taking photos of our cruise.

It was a beautiful day as the *Thames Maiden* made its way under the open Tower Bridge and down the river past Wapping Docks on the left, then the Surrey Commercial Docks on the right. Further along we passed Greenwich and the gas works. The river up to this point wound around some large bends, but straightened out as we passed Woolich. There was nothing much to see, except industry on both sides

A downstream composite three photo view along the Thames from the Hungerford Bridge showing L to R the Victoria Embankment, with St Paul's cathedral in the distance rising above Waterloo Bridge and on the left Festival Hall

The huge turrets of Windsor Castle that were visible as we approached Windsor

The author in the very extensive gardens of Windsor Park with the castle in the background

Grenadier guards strolling around Windsor gardens making sure everything is secure

Windsor on the Thames and the Castle turrets above the town

If I were to pass here at the time of writing however, I would have seen structures standing up above the river's surface. They are part of the Thames Barrier, which was completed in 1984 to protect London against floods and high tides in the Thames River. There had been occasions when these two factors coincided and parts of London were flooded. The last big flood was in February this year 1953, but the high water did not reach London. The level of the tides in the Thames has risen over the past two centuries, which has not helped the problem.

The Thames began to widen a little as we passed Tilbury Docks, which are large and deep enough to accommodate medium sized, ocean liners. The *Thames Maiden* left the river and entered the Thames Estuary, with the Isle of Sheppy and the town of Sheerness on our right. On our left, or north shore we passed by the popular and closest seaside beach town to London, Southend-on-Sea. The *Thames Maiden* was now in the open Thames Estuary approaching Margate in Kent on the edge of the North Sea, where the *Thames Maiden* pulled into a wharf to allow us to go ashore for an hour.

I had a wander around Margate and a bite to eat. Both Margate and Clacton, which I visited with the Stevenage mob, lie on the shores of the North Sea. Margate was not a beach town of the same standard or size as Clacton, the sand on the beach was rather dirty and the town ill kept.

The voyage back to London was very interesting, because as the *Thames Maiden* approached the Tower Bridge, we saw the drawbridge being raised just in front of our cruise ship. I was sure that this was done just for the benefit of the TV cameras, an added thrill to complete my very enjoyable, boat cruise down 'Old Father Thames that just keeps rolling along.' The cruise gave me a good look at a part of England that does not get much publicity.

Tuesday 4th August 1953: After work, I feverishly wrote letters during the evening to tell people I was about to leave England, and to thank those who had helped me in various ways, during my time abroad. A letter of resignation to the YCA, saying how much I enjoyed being a member. How much it had helped me learn about the politics and social life of the young people of London. I also wrote my resignation to Napiers, ready to hand in next Friday.

Wednesday 5th August 1953: After work I continued with my letters, writing special letters to May, Uncle John, Auntie Greta, Uncle Bob and Auntie Ruby, then a long letter to my parents. June Lucas rang and I arranged to have a drink with her next week.

Thursday 6th August 1953: I was invited over to Pam's flat, where I met Ralph, Nellie and Noel. We had a slashing meal of chicken and wine, then we went to the Six Bells Pub at Chelsea and drank ourselves merry. I thought that Nellie was a little lonely now with Netta gone, although she still had her daughter Noel and Pam close by. It was a great night together, but I was not sure what we were celebrating. My return to Australia, perhaps.

Friday 7th August 1953: I handed in my notice to Napier's to finish work the next Friday. No fuss, but with mixed regrets; because I had thoroughly enjoyed the experience and wished that it had been for a longer period. There was also the nagging thought that, because I had lied about the length of time I said I intended to stay at Napier's to get the job, any other Australians who sought work there, would be at a disadvantage. Not only that, but it did not enhance the reputation of Australians as being trustworthy people. However, I had learnt my lesson.

Chapter 29
A MUSICAL END TO MY LAST WEEKS IN ENGLAND

Saturday 8th August 1953: I went into the West End and met Ralph and Gladys at Ralph's surgery where he put a filling in my tooth. Then Ralph and I drove up to Stevenage in lovely sunshine. I lazed the day away in the sun, and in the evening we all went for a few beers in a pub in Codicote.

Sunday 9th August 1953: Another lovely day and more sun. Ralph drove me over to see Mac and his wife in Stevenage Newtown. Stevenage Newtown was on the leading edge of town development. Stevenage Newtown was designated as 'The UK's first Newtown in 1946.' It has been expanding ever since. Mac is a Cockney through and through, a rare, but great breed. He had been a very good friend to me at Kings in Stevenage. We had a cup of tea together and a long talk together, before I said goodbye to Mac and his wife. We wished each other good luck. Ralph thought they were a lovely couple.

I had the privilege of a first-hand look at the housing in the town and the development when I visited Mac and his wife. The old town, however, was not neglected but underwent many changes, which I believe has still retained its original character. The Great North Road had been replaced by the M1 motorway, which diverted all the intercity traffic around the town. It was indeed a joy for me to have been a temporary citizen of Stevenage.

Back at Brians, I went for a drink and a game of dart cricket for the last time at the Crooked Billet. After a superb lunch and more lazing in the sun we all went up to the Marquess of Grandby, for our last drinks together. Saying goodbye to Brian and Sheila, Jim and Jean, was a very sorrowful time for me. I thanked them all again and again for their wonderful hospitality, which I could never repay. I left some of my records with Sheila, saying that when they played them, I hoped they would be reminded of how grateful I had been for the good times they gave me and for their love and friendship. I would be seeing Ralph again before I left London.

In the afternoon I left Stevenage for the last time, sadly travelling back to London on the train past Kings under my 'Bridge of Serendipity.' I left Stevenage, with the belief that I could not have lived and worked in a better town and locality for the first three months of my two year stay in the UK. It had all worked out splendidly, way beyond anything I could have hoped for.

Monday 10th August 1953: The beginning of my last week at Napiers. After dinner Syd, one of the few friends I made at Bridges, came around to number 22. We spent some time up in my room talking about all manner of topics, including my work at Napiers and how it compared with working at Bridges. I told him about my life in Australia, my tours around the Continent and my proposed journey back to Australia. We then went around to his place and spent a while with his wife talking about their life in London, before I wished them both goodbye.

Tuesday 11th August 1953: I returned to the Royal Festival Hall, this time with Ralph, where we saw *The Nutcracker*, a grand ballet. Next on the program we saw Anton Dolin dancing Ravel's *Bolero* solo. Not for one moment was Anton Dolin's solo dance of *Bolero* boring, nor did it appear repetitive. Ralph had not been to the Royal Festival Hall before. He was suitably impressed and enchanted, not only by the ballet, but also by the splendour of the night time view of the Thames and London from the big windows of the hall, but also by Festival Hall itself. Once again, it was a truly wonderful night for my last night at the ballet, which provided me with so much enjoyment during the time I lived in London. It had been a very hot day, 89°F (32°C), a little like home in summer.

Wednesday 12th August 1953: I heard that there was a big railway strike in France, so that was going to be interesting. I planned to hitchhike anyway, but it was a bit of a worry nonetheless. I had tea with June Lucas and Joan Cooper. Afterwards we all decided to go to a prom concert at the Royal Albert Hall with some character named Bob, and a stuck up Aussie girl. It was a hot and sticky night again as we boarded the tube to South Kensington, the nearest station to the Royal Albert Hall of which I had no knowledge, or the Proms for that matter.

The Royal Albert Hall is a huge amphitheatre opened in 1871 in honour of Prince Albert, the Consort of Queen Victoria. It has a seating capacity of 5,000 persons as well as a large promenade area. There are a number of seats reserved for life, for people who first subscribed to the construction of the great hall. The Albert Memorial, a large statue of Prince Albert is situated in the park just across the road from the Hall. The Promenade Concerts commenced in 1941 from an idea of Sir Henry Wood, an English musician and conductor. He wished to bring orchestral music to the people of London, especially new works. .

The 'Prom' season lasts from mid-July to mid-September. It is a very popular, classical music event. I still have my programs setting out all the works that were to be played during that 59th

season. The orchestral works played that night were the *Hansel and Gretel Overture* by Humperdinck, a charming piece of music. I had seen the opera on TV a month or so ago. *Scheherazade for soprano and orchestra* by Ravel, and Elgar's *Symphony in E Flat*. After interval there were two works, *Concerto No.3 in D minor* by Rachmaninoff and finally *Dance Overture* by Alan Bush. The orchestra was the BBC Symphony Orchestra, the first half conducted by Sir Malcolm Sargent, the second half by John Hollingsworth.

At first I wasn't very impressed with the Royal Albert Hall, but the orchestra sounded really good. We bought tickets for the promenade area (standing) that only cost 2/6. I like to sit when I listen to music. I enjoyed all the music immensely, but did not like having to stand all the time during the playing of the works. The other option was to sit on the floor, but I am not a floor sitting person either. I discovered that the dearest seats were only 8/6.

Thursday 13th August 1953: I started packing, filling one case to the brim. Then I got on with the business of planning my route across France and Italy, which I had been putting off, maybe subconsciously because I really didn't want to leave. I decided I wanted to go to another Prom concert, but this time by myself with a seat, not standing. Looking through the program booklet, I found a couple of most unlikely works, which were on the following Saturday night. *Concerto for Harmonica and Orchestra,* and a *Romance for Harmonica*, with harmonica virtuoso Larry Adler as soloist. I decided to book a seat as soon as possible.

Friday 14th August 1953: My last work day at Napiers. At the end of the day I said goodbye to my workmates and picked up £6 odd as my final payment. In many ways I was sorry to leave Napiers as it was a great job, but this was another tie I had to break on my way back home.

I booked my seat for the proms and went around and picked up Pam. We went to Nellie's place where Pam, in a puzzling mood that night, said she wanted to get drunk! Where had I heard that before? We bought some bottles of beer at a pub nearby. After we had consumed a few beers, Pam told me to get a little girl to do Paris with. Pam brought out some dirty pieces of poetry from her handbag and recited them to us. I must admit, I felt a little uncomfortable. I did not expect that Pam, who I had just got to know, would be the sort of young lady to carry that type of stuff around in her handbag, let alone read them to me. Why did she have to disillusion me? However I walked her home and kissed her goodnight, returning to number 22 with my mind in a muddle.

Saturday 15th August 1953: I picked up all my traveller's cheques at the bank, as well as some French francs, a total sum of around £80 Sterling. Ma Banks left number 22 to go and stay at Barbara's for the weekend. I spent the day watching the cricket at the Oval on TV, packing and planning my final route to Naples, via the wonderful chain of youth hostels on the way.

After I made my dinner, I set out for the Royal Albert Hall, by myself this time thank goodness. It was a pity that Netta had left, because I am sure she would have enjoyed being there with me. I had a comfortable seat in the immense hall and listened enthralled to the various works played. The orchestra was The London Symphony Orchestra conducted by Basil Cameron. The first works were *'Overture, A Midsummer Night's Dream'* by Mendelssohn, *'Concerto No. 1 in E flat'* by Liszt, and *'Symphony No. 8 in B minor' (the unfinished)* by Schubert.

Then, the work I had really been waiting for. The first performance of the Australian born composer Arthur Benjamin's

Concerto for Harmonica and Orchestra. The concerto was announced by the conductor as the composer walked down the aisle with arms raised to the delight of the audience. When the clapping ceased, the small figure of Larry Adler appeared. He took up his position in front of the orchestra and the concerto, which Adler had commissioned, began. The huge comparison in sound level between the large orchestra and solo, chromatic harmonica (amplified), was wonderfully combined in a unique concerto of enjoyable music. The last work before interval was *Scherzo, L'Apprenti Sorcie* by Dukas.

After interval, and the first item, *Three Hornpipes* by Murrill. Larry Adler came back on stage to play on his harmonica, Vaughan Williams *Romance for Harmonica and String Orchestra.* This however, was not a first performance. It was very different piece of music to the concerto, with the accompaniment being only piano and strings. It was a very musical piece, much brighter than the concerto. I never believed I would witness a harmonica being played in such a setting. It was truly something to see and hear.

Grieg's *Incidental Music for Peer Gynt* brought the concert to a close. This music reminded me of Netta, and of the wonderful times we had spent together, skiing and at the theatre, because the very first time I met Netta was in Melbourne, this music was playing in the background of a hall, and she told me what it was. I bought a record of the Romance, which I still have on a 12 inch 78 rpm disc. If I had known about the Prom concerts I would have gone to many more.

Sunday 16th August 1953: I did some more packing and wrote a couple more letters. The strike in France was literally at a standstill. Allan Coillet, from our Rover Crew in Heidelberg, rang and I arranged to meet him at 2 p.m. at Liverpool Street Station. Barbara had invited me to lunch so off I went to Putney. We had a pleasant lunch together, talking about my life in London and my plans for the future. I told her how grateful I had been, to be part of the Banks family. How good her mother had been looking after me during my time at number 22. We parted with a big hug and a kiss and a firm handshake with Chris.

I met Allan at Liverpool Street Station. It was a great reunion because I had not seen him since I left the Rover Scouts and joined YHA in 1949. We walked up to Marble Arch and then wandered around the West End. We had a meal at a café and I took him back to number 22. We had the house to ourselves, as Ma was at Barbara's, and the Cornishes had moved out about a month ago. Allan had been to a Rover Scout Moot not far away from Bad Ischl in Austria, so we had lots to talk about. We watched TV for a while before we parted with a scout's, left hand shake.

Monday 17th August 1953: I finished packing, ready for the Orient Line to pick up my luggage and put it on board the *Orion,* when it left Southampton. I went into the West End and bought a couple of records (one of Larry Adler's), then out to Ralph's, where I had two teeth filled, my last dental work on National Health. Afterwards we went to the Star and Garter for a drink and a game of bar billiards, the last time Ralph and I would enjoy the convivial surrounds of the Crew's Quarters on a Monday night.

Tuesday 18th August 1953: The weather broke a bit this morning with a little rain. I met Ralph and a friend of his and we went off to see the fifth Test at the Oval. The cricket ground is immediately recognisable to TV viewers, by the gasometer behind the ground. The weather brightened up and we watched our Aussie blokes collapse horribly. It looked as though the Ashes would be England's. At the end of the game I wished Ralph goodbye and thanked him for his wonderful friendship. Ralph said it had been great for him to have me as a true Aussie mate. He said he would really miss me. He wished me a safe journey home and we vowed to keep in contact. I was so glad that I had introduced him to the nurses and my other friends, as he had done for me in Stevenage.

Wednesday 19th August 1953: The carrier came to collect my luggage. I watched the TV and saw the last day of the Test, when Compton hit Morris for four to end the match and win the series for England. The Englishmen went wild when the last wicket fell! They had won back the Ashes after 19 years. I did not begrudge their win in the year of the Coronation, it seemed appropriate.

Ma, Gwyn and Sylvia rang to say goodbye, but Chris wouldn't speak to me; because he was having an argument with Barbara. I thanked them all for their friendship. My last words were with Ma, who was very reticent, but she wished me well. I thanked her for being a mother to me and looking after me so well. I wished her all the best for the future.

My connection with the Banks family had come to an end. I was saddened and puzzled why, for the last of my four days in number 22, Mrs. Banks got out of the house and left me alone. Was it because for the time I was there, I was her son and she could not bear to face me to say goodbye? She had treated me like a son, even though we did have our disagreements.

I believe, she first went to Barbara's place, then I think to Sylvia and Gwyn's. She had no sons except her beaut son-in-law Gwyn. Her other son-in-law was hopeless. I would not have been surprised if Chris and Barbara's marriage didn't last much longer.

I climbed into bed for my last sleep in England, I was really disappointed because I would have liked to have said goodbye to Ma Banks personally and given her a big hug and kiss.

The Captain of the *Thames Maiden* being interviewed by the BBC

A BBC helicopter filming our cruise ship on the way to Margate

The Tower Bridge opened for the Thames Maiden to pass under at the end of the cruise

At the Oval to see the second last day of the 5th test

Brian and Ralph at the door of the Crooked Billet on one of my last days drinking at this quaint pub

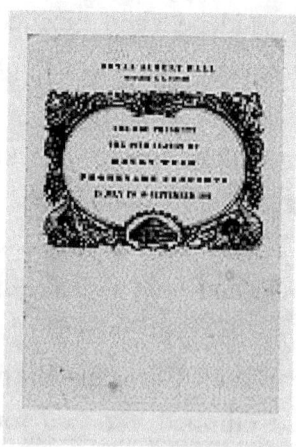

The Henry Wood Prom Concert program guide

Lots of other thoughts went through my mind as I lay there waiting for sleep to come. What a really wonderful time I had experienced in this great country. How friendly everyone had been to me when I lived in Stevenage and then in London. How exhilarating it was to be living in one of the most important cities in the world. How lucky I was to have been there at the time of the Coronation. Joining the Young Conservative Association and being a part of the group of friendly young people, not to mention the beautiful young women I met there and dated.

Dancing at the Hammersmith Palais became a venue nearby where I could go and relax, have a beer and listen to great band music, dance and never know who I would meet. During the time I lived in London and Stevenage, I met and dated quite a variety of English girls and learned a lot about the species. How satisfying it was to have Netta with similar interests to me, as a lovely Platonic friend. I would never forget my life as a Londoner, which would always be a part of my existence. Why, oh, why, didn't I think to invite Joan around to spend the night with me as she said she would? I supposed, because my mind was full of the next big step I was embarking on, the beginning of my journey back to Australia and home.

Thursday 20th August 1953: August 1953. I rose early on a very rainy morning and tidied up my room. I had my usual breakfast of cereal and then packed my rucksack. I had intended to buy a nice present for Ma, but when she walked out on me, I forgot about it. I was very disappointed that I was robbed of the opportunity of thanking her for looking after me so well during my time in London.

I left Ma Banks a short note with my food ration booklets for the coming months. I checked that I had everything I needed handy, my passport and rail ticket. I placed the front door key on the kitchen table and had a last look around my room to make sure I hadn't missed anything. I put on my rucksack, walked outside and closed the door of number 22 Chesilton Road for the last time.

IN REMEMBRANCE

I mourn the death of my beloved Queen Elizabeth II who passed away on Thursday 8th September 2022 age 96. She was of my generation and a wonderful inspiration to me during my long life

ABOUT THE AUTHOR

The author age 24

Gordon James Robert Smith. Author, historian and artist was born in 1927 in Victoria. He went to the Heidelberg State School and the Preston Technical School, and became a tradesman fitter and turner with the Victorian Railways (VR) in 1949. He was a member of the Boy Scouts, Rover Scouts and the Youth Hostels Association (YHA). Together with another YHA member he left Australia in 1951 to travel by ship to the UK on a working and backpacking holiday for two years. He returned to Australia in 1953. Soon after, in December 1953, he joined the SEC Kiewa Hydro-Electric Scheme and began watercolouring. In 1954 he married Dilys Terry and during his ten years on the Scheme, they raised a family of a girl and two boys.

In 1963 he and his family left the SEC and shifted to Melbourne where he worked for Australian General Electric (AGE) as a facilities engineer until AGE closed down in 1983. He then taught pneumatics and hydraulics at the Royal Melbourne Technical College (RMIT) until he retired in 1993 He played golf and skied for much of his life. After he retired he began writing many books about his life. He is now 95 and lives with his wife in Box Hill North.

The author age 90

BOOKS BY THE AUTHOR

Co-authored *Pneumatic Control for Industrial Automation,* published by John Wily. Self published books: *An Australian Backpacker Abroad 1951-1953-Mountains of My Youth-Working and Raising a Family On The Kiewa Scheme* and *Learning a Trade 1944 to 1949-20 Watercolours of the Kiewa Scheme.* He has published the following Ebooks on Smashwords. *Two Voyages-My Journey Through Occupied Austria 1952-To the Swiss Alps via Venice-The Assimilation Of An Aussie Backpacker-An Aussie Backpacking Londoner-Back to Australia via France and Italy-Concrete Hard Rock Earth and Snow-The High Plains Patrol.* The last books he completed include. *Come On Board* and *An Aussie Backpacking Londoner 1952-1953*, both published by Tale. Complete and to be offered for publication. *Backpacking by Train in Europe,* and *Skiing in Zermatt 1952*

www.ingramcontent.com/pod-product-compliance
Lightning Source LLC
Chambersburg PA
CBHW050311010526
44107CB00055B/2194